Happy Mother's Day
Lots of love from
John & Paddy
May 12, 2002

D1824462

NOT ALONE

NOT ALONE

Alwine Joan Franke

27/4/2002

Alwine Franke (signature)

The Book Guild Ltd
Sussex, England

First published in Great Britain in 2002 by
The Book Guild Ltd
25 High Street,
Lewes, East Sussex
BN7 2LU

Typesetting in Times by
Keyboard Services, Luton, Bedfordshire

Printed in Great Britain by
Bookcraft (Bath) Ltd, Avon

A catalogue record for this book is available from
The British Library

ISBN 1 85776 631 8

My sincere thanks to Michael, Christopher and Robin (who came after); to my husband Kurt of 55 years, my parents and brother and to my lifetime friend Joan Spinks who all gave me

Courage, Determination and Faith.

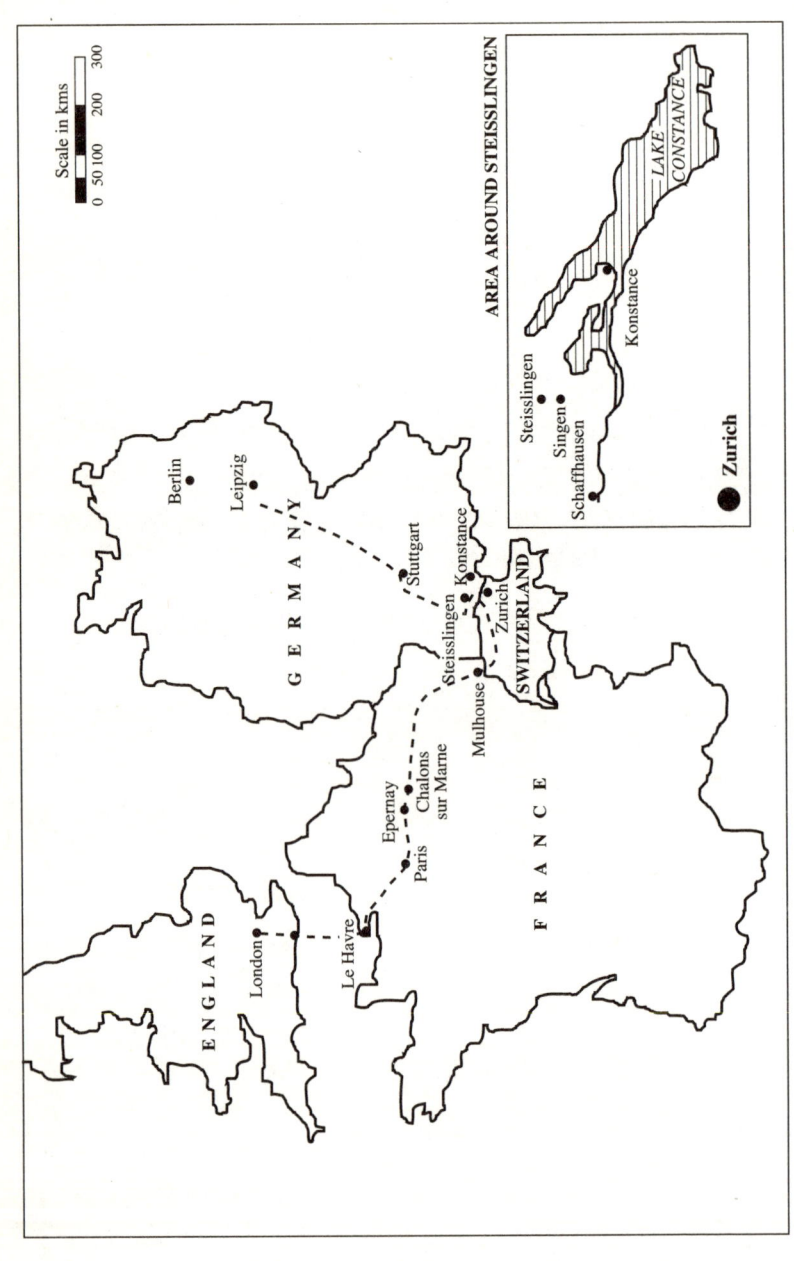

Scale in kms

0 50 100 200 300

AREA AROUND STEISSLINGEN

LAKE CONSTANCE

Steisslingen

Singen

Schaffhausen

Konstance

Zurich

Berlin

Leipzig

GERMANY

Stuttgart

Konstance

Steisslingen

Zurich

SWITZERLAND

Mulhouse

Epernay

Chalons
sur Marne

Paris

FRANCE

ENGLAND

London

Le Havre

PART ONE

1

September 4, 1939 – Leipzig, Germany

With one exception, fear, misery and despair showed on the face of every woman and child packed into the waiting room of police headquarters on the first floor of the building on Peterstrasse.

Now and again a woman sobbed, or a child whimpered, but in the main there was silence. The hard school of experience had taught them a stern lesson in the art of self-effacement in the last few years, and none of them wished to attract undue attention, for it could have very unpleasant consequences.

I was the exception. I carried a small suitcase, and although it wasn't very heavy, I shifted it every now and again from one hand to the other and flexed my fingers each time I did so.

Here, among the bowed shoulders, drab clothing and dull, lifeless looks, and with an effort which belied my fears, I carried my head high. My uncovered fair hair, slight build and deceptively calm outlook probably gave me a much more youthful look than my twenty-six years. Several of the jack-booted and uniformed German police turned their heads for a second look as they went about their business, pushing their way from room to room.

But my defiant carriage and steady look was an act; an act which I hoped I could carry through until it became a habit. Up to now I had never had to face up to a situation alone. There had always been someone to advise, comfort and give a hand where necessary. Perhaps it was this very fact which made me all the more determined to show a brave face.

Three days ago German tanks and troops had rolled and

marched into Poland, and amid the blaring of street loud-speakers and turned-up radios, the sound of which attracted groups of people to their doors to listen to the raucous voices announcing the news, I had gone about my business with a shrug of my shoulders. I was interested with the detachment of an onlooker. It was none of my business. I was *British*.

True, there had been a lot of talk of probable war, but I had pushed the rumours and the news from my mind as ridiculous. England and Germany, I thought, couldn't possibly become enemies, whatever propaganda indicated.

I was dreadfully wrong.

Yesterday the blow had fallen, and I had been forced to accept the hard facts of reality. England and France had declared war on Germany and all talk of peace for Europe had turned to the sour and acid taste of premonition.

Following the announcement of war, heavily printed notices appeared in the *Leipziger Allgemeine Zeitung*, and others had been tacked in prominent positions outside every official building, ordering all aliens to report to the police. The orders had been made public so swiftly that it was obvious they had been drafted in readiness and that the newspaper galleys had stood ready for rolling.

In 1939 I was living in a large rented room, part of an extremely clean and beautifully furnished apartment in a sub-urb of Leipzig. The owners were a kind couple named Herzog; the husband was a retired furrier. The only other occupant of this spacious accommodation was a maid, Erna.

It was she who brought me the news that there was war. It was evening, dusk was falling and that night seemed darker than ever. It took some time for the situation to move from unbelief to reality and when it did I knew with startling clarity that I was faced with a serious predicament. That fact filled my mind so that there was no thought left for the thousands who would have to face perhaps even greater challenges than I was to experience.

Nor, at the time, did I realise that there was another presence close to me who would be with me, and later with my children and me, throughout the war, keeping a ceaseless

4

watch over our safety and giving me strength to cope with the dreadful years to come.

I had to do something, and while it didn't occur to me that open postal communication between Germany and England might already have been severed, I wrote a tear-blotched letter to my parents. Never had I yearned for their comfort and love as I did during those dark night hours. Were they feeling the same as I? Were they wondering how they could get in touch with me? The questions went on and on and finally I crept out of the apartment with my letter and posted it. A futile gesture, for of course they never received it.

Back in the apartment, I took the first step from immaturity to maturity, from irresponsibility to responsibility. In other words, I grew up. My first decision was that there would be no more tears, they would be wasted energy.

First thing in the morning I packed a suitcase, fully expecting to be interned, and with that in hand, I made my way to the police station.

At the police station, the women and children waiting with me were mostly Jewish and there was no doubt in my mind that I was in a much better situation than they were.

The large waiting room, surrounded by doors leading to small offices, rapidly became stifling. Even when one of the police officers finally found time to push his way towards the window nearest to him and open it, there was little relief, for in the streets it was hot and humid, with the foreboding heaviness of impending storm.

I found myself squeezed between a grey-faced, ageing woman, who clutched her drab and ill-fitting clothes around her as if afraid she would have them snatched from her, and a young girl in her teens, who might have been pretty had she not been nagged with fear. I tried to edge between them in an attempt to get as close as possible to the door which bore the letters 'P-S', my surname being Schaedlich. Anything to shorten this long wait, and the uncertainty.

Most of the women and children with whom I had been standing for almost three hours now had a five-pointed yellow star of David sewn or pinned on their breasts, proclaiming their origin. The more I averted my eyes from those stars, the bigger they seemed to get, until they appeared to fill my vision, and the implication of them filled my veins with a cold running fear.

I shuddered and shifted my feet in the rather heavy brown brogues I had put on that morning as being the most service-able shoes I owned, and I moved my small suitcase from my left hand to my right. There wasn't much in the case, just a change of clothing, a couple of warm knitted sweaters and toilet articles, and my small leather bound copy of Maeterlinck's *Wisdom & Destiny*, which was to be my close companion and comfort throughout the war years. So it was not heavy, but there was no room to set it down on the floor and my hand was getting sore from carrying it for so long.

My efforts hadn't brought me any nearer to the door, and as I resigned myself to the fact that the police certainly weren't going to hurry themselves to accommodate me or anyone else, my thoughts transported me back to England.

What would Mum and Dad be doing now? Poor Dad! He'd been born not too far from where I was now. Short, tubby, cuddly Dad, he'd left his home in Gera in the Thüringian forest when he was seventeen to continue his apprenticeship in hotel management, and he had never been back. He couldn't even speak German properly any more, although he would never completely lose his accent. And Mum! Mum had never travelled. Even a long ago trip to the Goodwin Sands had made her seasick, so she always said.

I thought of the green hills and coppices of Shropshire where she had been born, and for a brief moment the hot room and the yellow stars faded away and I could see and smell the dew-damp mushrooms growing in the orchards, see the dark green waving branches of the trees overhanging the hollows, and the nostalgic loss rose up in an overwhelming pain.

I was brought back to the present when a warm but shaking hand was placed over mine. 'Don't cry, child! Don't cry!' It was the woman in the ill-fitting coat, trying to offer comfort, when she herself was so obviously in desperate need of it, perhaps even more than I was. I had been so transported in

6

spirit to my beloved England that I hadn't realised that I was weeping. Now, remembering my decision of the night before of 'no tears', I gave her a grateful little smile. This woman couldn't help but at least she had shown me that I wasn't alone in misery.

I squared my narrow shoulders again. I would *not* break my resolve – at least the officials were not going to see me weep.

'Next!'

The sharp order snapped out as the door ahead swung open. I hesitated because my knees suddenly seemed to be made of rubber, and somewhere deep in my stomach all my nerves were tensed into a knot.

'NEXT!' The voice was even more commanding and I moved through the door and closed it behind me.

All of a sudden my mind was a roaring nothingness resembling an inadequate piece of machinery, the cogs of which were violently slipping and failing to grasp a ratchet. It seemed to be hours that I stood there waiting behind the man who sat at a desk in the room. In fact it can only have been a few seconds, and in those seconds I made the effort to collect myself. Fear and panic had to be put behind me and this had to be dealt with. I stood my case on the floor and again unconsciously flexed my fingers. The man at the desk turned his close-cropped head and faced me.

'*Heil Hitler!*' His voice snapped like whipcord.

'Oh! ... er ... *Heil Hitler!*'

Embarrassment flooded my cheeks with a rosy glow. Never would I be able to use the outlandish greeting with the military zip and pep even civilians put into it. It was lucky he wasn't standing, I thought, or he might have raised his arm in salute and that was worse, rather like saying one's prayers in public. The thought made me smile.

'What are you smiling about, *Fräulein*?'

'It's as easy to smile as to cry,' I answered.

'What's that?' He pointed at my case.

'I thought I had better be prepared and bring some things ... I'm ready. Where do I go?'

'Go? Where should you go? For what were you prepared?'

'Aren't I going to be interned?'

Swinging one jackbooted leg over the other, he rested an elbow on a stack of papers on his desk and surveyed me with a quizzical lift of his brows.

'Interned? We don't intern women and children,' he said.

My eyes turned momentarily towards the door.

'Oh, those! They're Jews. You're British, aren't you?'

'Yes!'

'Well, you've got nothing to worry about.'

He swung himself back to the desk.

'Just answer these questions, *Fräulein*,' and as an after-thought... 'Your German's not bad. Been here long?'

'Nine months.'

'Could you speak the language before you came to Germany?'

'No.'

'Why not? Your father is German, isn't he?'

'He's stateless.'

'Born in Germany?'

'Yes.'

'Then he's German ... and so are you.'

'I'm British. I've got a British passport.' I held out the dark blue book with its gold lettering and coat of arms on the front. The signature of Lord Halifax inside the cover gave me an almost tangible feeling of security. The tips of my fingers whitened as I gripped the slim document tightly. Even in offering it to his sight I instinctively battled against giving it out of my possession, for it was very precious to me, particularly at that moment. The man waved it away.

'You are German. The child of a German father is German. That is the law.'

'It's not in England, and my father didn't register me at the German Embassy,' I answered.

'That's enough. You are not in England now.'

I had said as much as I dared, perhaps a bit too much. Would I ever learn to hold my tongue? Always impetuous – it had got me into trouble on more than one occasion, but never on such a level as this.

8

'Where are you living now?'

'Angerstrasse, with the Herzog family.'

'Hmm. Age?'

'Twenty-six. I was born in London on the twenty-first of December 1913.'

'You may return to your residence. But understand, you may NOT leave Leipzig, *Fräulein*. You will also report to this office each morning. You may go.'

As I stepped out of the door, he barked 'NEXT' ... and the elderly woman who had held my hand shuffled in and took her place.

I shuddered. I had heard what they did with Jews.

I pushed my way through the waiting crowd, ran down the stairs and stepped into the street, where in spite of the heat I felt as if I could breathe pure air again.

It was only a short ride on the streetcar back to my room, and there a study of a map of the city quickly showed that I would have no reason to overstep its boundaries.

In actual fact I should not have been alone, for my father's elder sister, Anna, lived in Leipzig with her husband and their son, Fritz, and her daughter, her husband and their two children, the Lippmanns, lived not too far from them.

For a few weeks when I first arrived from England I had lived with the Lippmanns, but it was an uncomfortable household to be in, for the husband was a member of the SS and the son was affiliated with the Hitler Jungvolk (Youth) group. It was for this reason I had moved into a place of my own, which hadn't endeared me to my aunt.

My father's youngest sister, Martha, lived in Gera, a weaving town in Thüringia, where my father had been born. There was no way I could visit her because of the present restriction, and in any case she had her own troubles. Her husband was a sick man and undoubtedly her sons, my cousins, would be called up shortly for military duty, if that hadn't happened already. There would be no point in even attempting to add to her load.

I dropped off my case at the apartment and boarded a tram for Gohlis, where I had worked in the export department of the firm of Springer & Moeller, paint manufacturers. No sooner had I reached my desk than I was sent for. Herr Daube, the manager, hardly glanced up as I entered his office.

'There's nothing for it, Miss Schaedlich ... you will have to leave.'

'But I can't. There's nowhere to go. I need this job.'

'*Ja! Ja!* This I know. But you ... you are English. You can't stop on here. The circumstances, you understand? It's war.'

His eyes slid past my own and stopped at the edge of his huge mahogany desk, just short of my twisting hands. I couldn't help thinking that a short while ago, the officer at the police station had said I was German and that now Daube, in turn, was saying I was English...

'I'm not. I'm certainly not at war. You all know me. I have a contract. It doesn't run out for another two months.'

Here was a man with whom I had worked for six months, old enough to be my father, someone I had relied on to help me over the little wrinkles and difficulties which crop up in everyday living in a foreign country. He just couldn't let me down like this.

Besides, he too had left Germany when he was quite young, as my father had done, and he too had married an English woman. The one child of his marriage was a son, born in exactly the same circumstances as myself. His father was German, his mother English, and he, in accordance with British law, was British, as I was; except for one difference, he had been registered at the German Embassy at birth, whereas I had not, and probably Herr Daube, having gone to England much later than had my father, was not stateless.

The Daube family had returned to Germany during the years between the two wars and the son, because of that registration, was now eligible for the German Army.

'Perhaps you can get back to England,' suggested Herr Daube as he finally raised his eyes and took in my trembling lips and white, bewildered face.

There could be no redress – his words had a finality about them. Now I had no means of support. I would have to sit down and budget my meagre funds, most of which would have to be set aside to cover my rent if I was to retain a roof over my head.

Without replying I turned away, collected my personal things from my desk and walked from the room. I was followed by the gaze of those with whom I had worked for six months. It may have been just as well that I didn't stop to say goodbye, for I had no doubt that while many of the clerks and apprentices would have felt sympathetic, there were others who would have, since yesterday, turned from friendship to antagonism.

As I walked wearily down the stairs to the outside door, there were running footsteps behind me. I turned. It was the white-coated figure of Paul Broglie, a big, six-foot-six Swiss boy, one of the apprentices.

'Just a minute! Let me speak with you.'

'There's nothing you can do – nothing anyone can do.' My voice was flat and dull.

'Perhaps there is. How about this evening? After work?'

Without waiting for a refusal, he fished a pencil from behind his ear.

'What's your address? I'll be there about six o'clock.' He raised his right eyebrow in a quizzical attempt at being light-hearted and added, 'You don't mind, do you? Or would your landlord object?'

'No, Paul! I don't think he'll mind, and I certainly won't. Angerstrasse, number 7. I rent a room on the ground floor. The Herzogs' apartment. You'd better get back upstairs, you know what Herr Daube is like if you waste a minute.' I turned and left.

It had been a hot summer and although the morning had been sunny and clear, as I stepped onto the streetcar which would take me from the industrial quarter to my room near the centre of the city, I noticed dark clouds had started massing above the buildings, pressing down the air, so that the people on the pavement seemed to be cringing within themselves, unable to differentiate between the atmosphere and fear of the future, for even those free to go about their business seemed to sense coming disaster.

11

At this time of day there were few people on the streetcar and the few there appeared to be sitting as far from each other as possible, humped and defeated.

There was no one in the apartment when I got there. I went into my room and locked the door after me. Then, with no thought to my resolution not to weep, I threw myself on to the white-covered bed and collapsed face down and sobbed. On and on I whimpered as the tears flowed unrestrainedly down my cheeks, until at last, as exhaustion overcame me, I slept. When I awoke, it was just after four o'clock. My face was hot and damp from contact with the tear-wet bedspread, my hair was dishevelled and my face, when I looked in the mirror, was almost unrecognisable, with swollen red eyelids and nose. Worst of all, I realised this wasn't just a nightmare. The situation was only too real. First of all I had to repair the ravages of my outburst; under no circumstances would I allow anyone to see my weakness.

At six o'clock punctually, I opened the door to Paul. It needed no word from him for me to be aware that his morning's optimism had gone.

'I've to return to Switzerland,' he said. 'All officers have been recalled.'

'Recalled? Officers?'

'We have conscription in Switzerland. I did my service before I started my apprenticeship.'

He grasped my hand and looked down at me gravely. Then, stressing each word as if the emphasis must convince me, he added, 'Come with me ... from there you could get back to England.'

'Wouldn't that be running away?'

'Running away from what?'

'I ... I just don't believe this war will come to anything. It can't ... Mum's English and Dad's German ... at least he *was* German ... Oh dear, I can't go over all that again.'

I felt my resolve crumbling and turned away from him to angrily scrub off a tear which threatened to spill over.

'You'll be foolish if you don't try to get out ... I can assure you of that. Joan, you must listen to me ... you must.'

The pleading use of my name almost shook my resolution to stay, but not quite.

'Give me time, Paul. It's all so sudden. The whole thing has come tumbling down. I've got to think.'

'I'm sorry. I can't even give you time. I have to leave tonight. If you are coming, you'll have to come now, and even now, it'll be touch and go that the borders won't be closed.'

'I suppose so, and I'm probably wrong and stupid, but I can't go. Look! I'm sorry you are going, but I can't run. I'll stay here and see it out.'

In reality it wasn't that I was worried about running away, it was that I just couldn't face up to the danger of going at such a time, and had no conception of the far greater dangers I was to have to confront in the future. Paul shrugged and moved towards the door.

'Wait a minute, Paul, I'll come with you to the station.' I grabbed my hat and purse and we left the building and headed into the darkness of the streets.

There were no lights from the windows and no street lamps were lit. Black-out. Not many people were around and those we passed shuffled by like black, mysterious silhouettes.

The huge Leipzig *Hauptbahnhof* was a bustling contrast to the almost empty streets. Dimmed lights hung high above the platforms, giving a ghostly appearance to would-be passengers, who scurried about carrying their own baggage. There wasn't a porter in sight.

'Paul! What about your luggage?' I whispered, for the eerie atmosphere made me feel creepy.

'I left it ... no point. Might be glad to have empty hands when I get to the frontier.' He knew his words would frighten me, make me even more afraid than I was already, but he must have still hoped that I would change my mind.

I only answered softly ... 'Oh!'

At the ticket office he had to show his passport before he was given a ticket.

'Swiss? You may just make it, sir!'

And then, almost before I could think again, I was at the

barrier, and Paul lifted me to my toes and kissed me on the forehead.

'Take care, Joan! Take care!'

He pushed a piece of paper into my hand. 'There's my address. If you can write at all, write there and I'll try and contact your parents.'

With that he was gone. I raised my hand and touched the place where the brief kiss had landed. It had been a gentle, but all too much a final gesture.

Back in my apartment I sat with my elbows resting on the table, my chin on my hands. In the silence I turned inward on myself, mentally building up a wall around my heart. I was fully conscious that I had to find strength, a strength which might keep me from losing my sense of balance through what I hoped would only be days ahead.

It was as well that I could not know that the days would develop into months, the months extend into dreary lonely and often even more frightening years. I moved a few inches forward to the window and peered upwards between the buildings. The pending storm had passed over. It had probably moved in the direction of Magdeburg, leaving Leipzig as hot and airless as it had been earlier that day. Or was it already tomorrow?

With a sigh I got up, put an electric water heater into my brown teapot and took out a small packet of tea. There wasn't much left in the packet and I hoped the grocer across the road would have some more. A dismal hope, where would he get more supplies?

As I sipped the weak, milk-less brew, I thought how history was repeating itself. First Dad isolated in a foreign country and now me, I mused.

He, apprenticed as a waiter in Gera when he left school, had allowed the urge to travel to lead him from Germany in 1900 to work his way through France to England.

I remembered him telling me that when he was only seventeen, he had stood at a window of a drab hotel overlooking the English Channel and wept because he was alone and afraid of the future. He'd been worse off, for he understood no word

14

of the country where he had found work, and where eventually he had made his home.

Undoubtedly he had dreamed of returning some day – a dream which was never realised, for he died at the age of eighty-five without ever setting foot in his homeland again.

History was repeating itself in my case and I, too, dreamed that I would be able to return to England. In fact my painful feelings and thoughts must now be the same as his had been as he stood looking over the grey waters dividing him from the main continent and his home.

I remembered how eagerly he had questioned me when I returned in 1938 from a two-week vacation spent in his home town of Gera. Now I understood. In the midst of all the strangeness of another country, he must have yearned all the rest of his life to be back again in the old familiar streets, among his beautiful Thüringian hills.

Dad had never talked much about those years between the time he landed in England and 1911, when he married my mother. Working as a waiter, his intentions were to learn all he could of the hotel business and then go to California to continue his career. But that, too, was never to happen.

Instead he met a Church Army captain who befriended him. At a church in Marylebone he made other friends and interested himself in church work. His language problems must have resolved themselves fairly quickly, because in 1909 he was speaking for the church in public. Mother used to tell the story of how they had met.

While walking in Hyde Park on a Sunday evening with her older sister, they stopped to listen to a man conducting a Church Army service at Speakers' Corner.

'Don't you love his accent?' my mother asked her sister. 'He says "dis" and "dat" instead of "this" and "that".'

The next week she visited the church in Marylebone and she, too, became interested in its work. She had studied opera singing and had a beautiful soprano voice. It was in the choir, where my father was already singing, that they finally met officially. A loaned bible with a strategically hidden photograph within its pages brought them closer, and in 1911 they were married.

Shortly after this he had taken another apprenticeship as a hairdresser and barber. My mother's eldest sister loaned him the money to start up a hairdressing and tobacconist's shop in Fulham Road, London. It was over this shop that I was born.

A year later, war broke out and mobs of roughs took that opportunity to indulge in smashing and looting shops and businesses owned by Germans. My father was well-liked by his customers and when Fulham Road became their target, a customer came at night and warned him to get my mother and me from the living quarters above the shop and go to my mother's eldest sister's home in Kensington. We learned afterwards that the customers had stood shoulder to shoulder around the shop and prevented the bullying attack.

But this didn't save my father from the loss of his business, for in 1914 he was interned at Islington and during that time my mother and I lived on the charity of her sister.

For four years all we saw of Dad was during the short monthly visits we were allowed in the internment camp, and those visits were filled with apprehension for, as we neared the camp, groups of hoodlums were gathered on the corners near the gates, throwing at us anything they could lay their hands on, and shouting abuse, calling us 'German vermin'.

When Dad was released in 1918, he had to struggle to build a new livelihood, for the shop had become one of the casualties of war. There was, therefore, little time or inclination to teach me his mother tongue.

My only knowledge of German was a sentence learned parrot fashion from the one-page letters he was allowed to write from the internment camp. Across the centre of each letter was printed in heavy black print '*NICHT ZWISCHEN DIE ZEILEN SCHREIBEN*' (Do not write between the lines).

My mother told me that I would point a pudgy finger at the words and whisper them repetitively, not from recognition or understanding, but from having heard them from her when she said them over and over, in sadness, at the small space allowed for communication.

16

Perhaps I was, even at that early age, trying to reach some inner understanding with my father. Because of our situation I had hardly any physical contact with him. The one-hour visit allowed each month was all too brief; what could a father communicate to a child in an hour, devoted of necessity to discussion with my mother as to how we were to exist with our main support denied us? Beyond a fleeting caress and a kiss, I doubt if I ever realised during those first four years what a father really could be.

My thoughts leaped the years to a fortnight's holiday in Germany when I was twenty-five. Curious to get to know and see my father's country, I fell in love with it in those two weeks.

My father's younger sister, Martha, with whom I stayed, looked very like him, short, stout and round-faced. She lived with her husband and three children, Ilse, Rudi and Gerhard, in an apartment not far from the street where Dad had been born.

She had made me very welcome, even though their means were extremely limited, and because all the family were working I was left to myself to roam around and re-live my father's childhood.

Even in the evenings the family was occupied, for to swell their meagre income, they worked every spare minute, poking little cork discs into tiny toothpaste caps. I suppose it was lucrative, but they had to work terribly fast to make money, for it required 2,500 caps to bring in the equivalent of twenty-five cents.

My holiday over, I made up my mind that I would return to Germany and learn to speak the language.

It was for this reason that in 1939 I returned for an intended period of six months, which I thought should give me sufficient time to achieve my purpose.

It didn't take so long, though, for after three months, during which time I had lived with the Lippmanns, I understood hardly a word of what was going on around me. Then one day, as I was sitting reading and the radio was playing, irritatingly loudly, the music stopped and Hitler began to speak. I then

17

realised I had learned more from listening to those around me than I had thought, for I found I had a limited understanding of what he was bellowing.

At almost that same time I obtained a contract for six months' work in the paint factory of Springer & Moeller. This meant that the date of my return to England, set to take place after another three months, had to be postponed until the contract had expired; a series of good intentions which now resulted in my being caught in the net of war.

As I sat there, I realised that there would be no communication between my parents and myself until the war ended and my wishful thinking wasn't going to bring that event any sooner.

In the following years, apart from Red Cross letters allowed between the two countries, each with only its permitted twenty-five words, Paul was to be the only flimsy link connecting me with my parents, and I only dared use Paul's kind assistance in that direction about three times during the whole of the war year.

2

A review of my limited finances clearly showed that I would have to make some plans, and make them soon. Sufficient rent for two months was a priority, to safeguard my immediate future. It didn't leave much over and I immediately started to search for work.

This was a real endurance test. I walked. I walked through sunshine, through rain and inevitably and eventually, as winter closed in, through snow.

Upon looking back, I wonder if this was not training for what was to come. There seemed no work available, particularly for anyone with my qualifications, and, of course, with my nationality. Each application was rejected.

To relieve the tedium of plodding wearily through the snow, I sang softly to myself all the many Christmas carols I could remember. This served two purposes. Firstly it gave me something to think about, and thus a mile, instead of being measured in steps, was measured by five, six or even seven carols, depending on their length. Secondly, it served as an opportunity to think about home. Memories! Had it not been for them, perhaps I would never have survived, mentally at least. In the next few years, I was to dwell a great deal in the past.

It became possible to travel quite a distance by imagining myself back in the assembly hall at West Kensington Central School, where I had attended from the age of eleven, choosing and singing carols from the book given us by our class mistress, Miss Bryant. It even became a challenge to remember the order of the carols in the book. With its familiar red cover, it is still one of my treasured possessions. The sound of the English words linked me to the rapidly disappearing threads of my past life.

The words were real, but my existence seemed to have no reality. Singing kept up my spirits and, even more important, kept my mind to some extent off my tired and frozen feet, as I slipped and slithered on my way.

I hoped my shoes would hold out, for I had no boots to cope with the very often deep snow and there was no means of getting new footwear or of getting old ones repaired.

The walk from the city centre to the Angerstrasse was very beautiful both in summer and winter. The buildings of the Ring (the layout of the city of Leipzig is based on the wheel, the centre being the hub and the outskirts radiating like spokes) and the smooth lines of the Frankfürther bridge, with its well-kept park and rose terrace along the bank of the River Elster, were lovely, even now when they were covered with snow. In my loneliness, it was a frigid and sad beauty.

I'd almost given up hope of finding work, when one day as I passed through the street door of the building in Peterstrasse where the police headquarters were situated, I happened to notice a small shield, which until now had escaped my attention. 'BERLITZ SCHULE', I read.

Quickly I climbed to the third floor and was interviewed by Dr Petersen, who was in charge of this particular branch.

'Have you taught English before?'

Momentarily I hesitated, and then my desperate state gave balance to the lie. 'Yes! I have taught English to foreigners in England.'

Luck was with me. His English teachers had fled when war broke out and Dr Petersen needed help very badly. Even so, I was told that my case must first go before the education authorities.

There was a lapse of a few days and then a telephone message from Dr Petersen advised me to come to discuss matters further. He was holding a letter when I entered his office and told me that the chief concerns of the education authorities were my papers confirming my experience.

Schooled in the past weeks to think somewhat more quickly than usual, I answered with crossed fingers and a mentally recorded prayer, linking superstition with fervency.

'They are in England. I can't get them, of course, because of the war.'

Neither they, nor I, could prove the truth of the situation and I got my job and much needed salary.

It wasn't easy, this adjustment; the hours were from eight in the morning until nine at night, with three-quarters of an hour for lunch, during which time all the shops were closed.

This precluded buying food on any day but Saturday, when we only worked until four o'clock. We were not overpaid either at 20 marks – about £10 – a month plus a little extra for classes of six or more pupils.

That first year I lived almost exclusively on a diet of potatoes and tomatoes boiled together in one pot, often my only meal of the day. It was quick, and that adjective also applied to the rate at which I lost weight. It might also be well to explain that this was no recipe as such, nor would a cookery book writer have thought the result worthy of mention. The reason for this particular dish was a hot-point apparatus with one element and the possession of only one saucepan.

I supplemented the diet with the addition of an 'off point' soup, which I obtained on rare occasions at one of the local restaurants at lunch time. This soup, which had little, if any, nutrition, had two advantages. I neither had to cook it, nor had I to watch it cook. All the jokes about soup being dishwater, or the water in which socks had been washed, were embodied in that soup, plus a few others it would have been unwise to think of and less agreeable to mention.

But it made a change and eliminated washing up, on my more exhausted days. It was a thin vegetable soup, and as the Germans say, 'there were more eyes looking into it than looking out of it,' meaning that there were no fat globules floating on it.

As all food was rationed, any meal taken in a restaurant was subject to the presentation of ration cards; except, of course, this soup, which was a clear indication of its calorie value. Otherwise, in accordance with the meagreness or luxury of the meal taken, the waiter snipped off so many meat, bread and/or fat coupons. This, of course, necessitated an addition to the

21

waiter's uniform of a pair of scissors dangling from his apron strings.

These ration cards, each different in colour, were a marvel of organisation. Brown for bread; which included black bread, a few white rolls, flour, and luxury of luxuries, a few cake coupons. Blue for meat, and it was as well in those days to be on friendly terms with the butcher, who was probably driven to distraction by the constantly recurring plea, seldom heard these days, 'May I have a piece of really *fat* meat please?' or 'Could you spare me a little extra bone for soup?'

Following the war I could feel my hackles rise when I heard women complaining that they couldn't eat fat meat, or arguing with a butcher because he had included bone in their order.

Invention was the order of the day. Liver sausage was made of onion and sage with not even the smell of liver in it, coffee was made from ground roasted peas or acorns, and it was nothing short of miraculous to see the soups and other dishes produced. Shades of Mrs Beeton and her classic recipes starting with 'Take a dozen eggs...' The first sentence in each of *our* home-made recipes was: 'Place a pot half-full of water on the stove.' To that we added what was to hand, cabbage, carrots, potatoes, salt and a lot of imagination.

The blue meat ration card included, as well as a small ration of fresh meat, coupons for sausage. These rations were so infinitesimally small that while they delighted the palate for the first week of the month, they only too quickly disappeared, leaving anticipation for the next month's ration in their wake.

Those were not the only problems, though; perhaps the greatest was queuing up, sometimes for hours, waiting for a shipment of even rationed goods to arrive at a shop. Quite often, too, having waited patiently, it was nothing to arrive at the door of the shop to be told that stocks had run out until the next hoped-for shipment.

Children were often given a piece of bread with a round of sausage balanced on the near end. The trick was to bite the bread and, without taking the sausage, push it forward. The last mouthful, which included the delicacy, was savoured slowly and in thought, if not in deed, it was felt a complete sausage sandwich had been eaten.

There were also cards for fats, including butter, in very small quantity, margarine, cooking fat and oil. The only way to get any benefit from the oil was to put it in a bottle and save it. In a period of possibly four months, there would be just sufficient to pour on a good-sized salad – that is, if one had the wherewithal for a salad.

In this system of rationing, there was a practice frowned on by government departments. Perhaps one could not blame the food retailers entirely, however, as it is quite possible that, initially, they too were subject to a form of blackmail and merely passed it onto shoppers in self-preservation. I refer to the fact that now and again the Food Commission endorsed the issue of two or three oranges to each child, or, even more rarely, a lemon. Once word spread that a consignment had arrived at a local grocery store, queues of women and children lined up for hours to buy the treat. More often than not, when they finally arrived at the counter they were told that in order to receive the fruits they must also buy perhaps five pounds of parsley root, or whatever surplus, and usually almost useless, items the wholesalers had seen fit to unload on the retailer if he were to get his own allowance of oranges or lemons for distribution.

Utilising such a large quantity of parsley roots as flavouring became more and more sickening.

There was a card for milk, skimmed and blue; another for groceries such as oats, pearl barley, and yet another for soap. Who has not heard of that soap and its possible origins? With texture like stone, it was grey, and after washing, one wiped up the splashes of chalk spots where the droplets had fallen.

It may not be encouraging to present-day advertisers of the cream-like smooth and scented concoctions obtainable to preserve my lady's complexion, but frankly, although the stuff was unpleasant and harsh to use, it didn't appear to make any difference to the texture of the softest and most tender of skins, or perhaps we just had no time to notice.

For the washing of clothes, more often than not wood-ash

was employed. This didn't seem to matter so much in open country areas where the washing could hang in the open air, but in the cities, where, for lack of space most clothing was hung up in the attics to dry, the results were that clothes became dingier and dingier after every wash.

It is inevitable that the inhabitants of any other country believe that it is impossible for the English to live without numerous cups of tea. This was proven by the kindness of the grocer who operated at the rear of my apartment block, in a small alley.

When I went for my rations the first month, he produced from some obscure corner a hidden-away tin containing a pinch of tea, 'for the English lady'. I was grateful for it and was amazed at how long this pinch lasted. In the manner of the parable of the loaves and fishes, that tea stretched. There was no spoonful per person and one for the pot; but rather about ten tea-leaves just for the pot. Drowned in water and well stewed, it was delectable. Dried and served again with the next boiling, the quantity did double duty.

Eventually the grocer's welcome gift petered out, for tea was not included on ration cards. It disappeared entirely from the groceries and reappeared only in apothecary stores, to be issued under prescription from a doctor. Even coffee, the national drink, was only issued under rare, stringent conditions and then in minute quantities.

One evening as I was sitting alone in my room, working on the next day's lessons, there was a discreet tap on the door and Erna entered. 'I've just made some potato pancakes, *Fräulein*, would you like one?'

I needed no second invitation. This was to be a feast day. And the pancake proved to be delicious. I had no opportunity to thank her for a couple of days, and when I did see her she asked me if I had enjoyed the treat.

'Wonderful, Erna, very tasty!'

'Yes, I thought so too. Frau Herzog had a bottle of horse oil given her, so I was able to cook them in that.'

My mouth dropped open and I made a beeline for the bathroom, where I was sick. Poor Erna. I imagine she was somewhat confused to understand how a pancake so long ago digested could be causing all that trouble. *Horse oil*? I still shudder at the thought.

In spite of a regime which had, to all intents and purposes, abolished class distinction, it rapidly became apparent that war had changed more than the housewife's weekly marketing.

Before the war, the height of luxury in a restaurant had been music, and the lower class eating places had been without entertainment. Now, money made no difference. A war had given rich and poor alike the same status. Everyone had the same food cards and even the poorest meals could be eaten in luxurious surroundings, with the added piquancy of an orchestra.

Where an orchestra had been depleted owing to enlistment, the plaintive tones of a single zither or violin accompanied the frugal meals. In spite of this, restaurant meals were not economical ration-wise and they were only indulged in on very special occasions.

3

At the Berlitz School, the lesson 'hour' consisted of fifty minutes. The ten minutes before the hour were solely our own. A room was reserved for the teachers for this ten-minute recreation, which turned it into a veritable Tower of Babel.

The room was small, oblong in shape, about nine feet by five feet, and in this space the teachers congregated. Two Italians; a Spaniard, who appeared to speak every language under the sun, for he could switch from one conversation to another without difficulty; a French woman, full of complaints and gestures; a charming white-haired White Russian lady; the German Principal, Dr Petersen, and his daughter Mia. She was a fair-haired, tall and aloof girl and acted as co-secretary with a girl named Lala Fritz, who was round, roly-poly, dark haired and full of merriment. Mr White and I were the English teachers.

Mr White was a character. I met him for the first time when I went from our third-floor accommodation to report to the police offices on the second floor. He stood at the counter, on the same errand. The officer in charge nodded towards him and whispered to me, 'He's English too.'

He looked from one to the other of us, waited a moment then said, 'You English! I forget you have to be introduced before you'll speak to each other.' This made us smile in spite of ourselves and we shook hands.

As we left the office, Mr White told me about himself. Seventy-four years of age, he had lived in Germany most of his adult life, working as a translator. He had begun this career long before the First World War, at the outbreak of which he had enlisted in the British Army, thereby losing his job and having his finances in Germany confiscated. After the war, he returned, started his career anew and married.

At the outbreak of this war, his bank account had been frozen, only sufficient being allowed him to pay rent, insurance, taxes and the minimum necessary for food. I suggested that he, too, should apply to the school to teach English. He did this, and, his qualifications proving adequate, he was allowed by the education authorities to start immediately.

Of medium height, with white hair, very lean and slightly bent, he wore glasses, behind which his eyes twinkled mischievously. His sense of humour was most refreshing.

We had many discussions about past and present politics in our short recreation periods and it was just as well that there was no eavesdropping apparatus installed in that room. I did wonder, however, how the sounds from a microphone would have relayed, for the jabber of different languages must have emerged as the most amazing and noisy gibberish.

Surprisingly enough, in this free ten minutes each hour, I managed to embroider quite a number of table and teacloths on the occasions, usually in the evenings, when Mr White was not there.

There was little time for thought or brooding. One just lived, and not even from day to day, for with the uncertainty of events and regulations, it was closer to living from minute to minute.

My pupils ranged in age from two Italian children of seven and eight years old to an elderly man of sixty-four. Some of the pupils took private lessons, some lessons were confined to two persons, and others to classes of up to ten. Some were quick to learn, some were slow. The majority seemed to expect us to walk in with a bucket of English and a syringe, and syphon the language into them. It was hard work, but it answered its purpose. Three of my pupils went to England after the war and passed their English at Cambridge University.

Mary and Ralf Hoeckner, the two Italian children, were imps and never above playing a joke on me. One day as I sat down at the table I found a text book inverted in a 'V' in front of me. When I picked it up, I was horrified to see a pile of maggots crawling under it. Ralf, who had collected them to feed his bird at home, thought this very funny and giggled throughout the lesson. Some days, I found a caricature of me chalked on the blackboard when I entered the room. Ralf was a tidy artist with a flair for humour.

Little Ursula Herbst, a shy and timid child of twelve, made a request that she only be taught by me, because she was too nervous to be given instruction by a man.

Christine Walther, now married and with a child of her own, was the quiet and studious type, who gave no trouble at all and was a joy to teach. Despite a number of younger brothers, who she helped her mother to raise, she never came without her lesson being prepared.

Another delightful pupil was the daughter of an actor and actress, both appearing in opera at the Leipzig Opera Theatre. She came to school solely for the pleasure of being able to sit down and read Shakespeare's plays with me. Those were the hours I cherished most. Always an avid reader, as a child of twelve I would sneak my father's beloved copy of Shakespeare's complete works up to my bedroom, where I read well into the small hours of the morning, with the aid of an electric torch under the blankets.

Those 'lessons' were cherished and as a consequence the minutes flew by much quicker than the everyday grind of teaching.

Towards the end of my teaching career in 1941, the German Army had begun to send officers to us for tutoring in English, and mild sabotage on the part of Mr White was a glorious joke to us both. Whether they learned anything that would have done the officers any good or aided them in the furtherance of their duties would be a moot point. Dialects, complete nonsense, and rude words, none of them were beneath the use of Mr White in his efforts to prevent them learning anything which would enable them to translate more than the simplest of sentences. Any school English they had, while it had been well taught and learned, was by rote and translation, which was of no use when they tried to speak or understand the spoken word. Conversational English had not been taught, and as the Berlitz method was conversational, it was a case of starting from the beginning again.

Mr White did a good job in his own way; on my part, when

following up on one of his lessons, I had much ado to keep a straight face at the use of some of the expressions and words which were addressed to me, in the most serious and courteous manner, by the students. Some were of an extremely Rabelaisian nature.

It leaves little to the imagination as to the self-control I had to exercise, when approached with dignity, and while gravely shaking hands, with a serious and fervent member of the class, as he practised his lately learned lesson. 'Good morning, madam. I trust you are well – what a pity it's bloody well raining', or, when a too apt pupil came in shivering from the snow outside remarked in carefully selected words that 'It's enough to freeze the —'

Possibly, however, the height of curious courtesy was that with which a youth who, having first made detailed enquiry of Mr White as to the correct procedure when excusing himself from a lady, stood to attention and, politely bowing from the waist, requested solemnly, 'Excuse me please, I have only one bladder.'

My indignation on this occasion was met with the utmost seriousness of expression on the part of Mr White. He looked over his spectacles and said dryly, 'Well, he was right, wasn't he?'

One of my pupils was the son of Goerdeler, the former *Bürgermeister* of Leipzig. Probably the plot to assassinate Hitler was already being planned, for no doubt Goerdeler, who was deeply involved in it, hoped that afterwards he and his family could escape to England. His wife and daughter were already conversant with the English language; but the boy, who was a likeable though pimply and clumsy-mannered youth of about fifteen, was not particularly gifted.

He, of course, never had the opportunity to travel; for after the assassination attempt, his father was caught and later hanged, and the whole family, as a result of his activities, disappeared. Many in those days disappeared without a trace and curiosity was dangerous. While many considered, or speculated privately, no one in the school enquired or ever mentioned the boy again.

Most of my spare time was very lonely. I often sat looking out of the window of my room at the unprepossessing wall of the next door buildings, trying to think myself into the family circle at home and wondering what they were doing. Or I transferred my troubled thoughts to paper in the form of poetry. Good, bad or indifferent, it was of little consequence. The blank pages were mute recipients of my innermost feelings and acted as a safety valve to nerves already stretched to breaking point.

I also read quite a lot, and made friends with Mrs Toni Mahler, who owned a private lending library. Quite a bit of my time, when I had no lessons, was spent with her, classifying and sorting her English section, which was far more extensive in my experience than that of a foreign section in libraries of any English-speaking country.

Our acquaintanceship, however, was confined solely to our book interest and the precincts of her library. In those days of the war and with a government under which one careless word was sufficient to cost one's freedom, it was rare indeed to gain anything nearly approaching an intimate friendship, even with those with whom one was in constant touch.

My great standby was a small green, soft leather-bound copy of Maeterlinck's *Wisdom & Destiny* given me by a dear friend for my twenty-first birthday. In my most depressed moments I turned to this book, not for solid reading, but to pick out sentences and paragraphs which provided comfort and brought philosophical peace to my confused thoughts. I still refer to this edition, with its underlined phrases and marginal notes. It is a well-worn, well-loved, old friend.

Occasionally pupils invited me to eat with them in different *Gasthäuser* or restaurants. There were several university students still enjoying liberty as civilians, as not all had been called to the front at that time. In those early days of the war, some of them were given a short reprieve in order to complete their degrees. One of these young men knew the cook in the Ratskeller, a restaurant situated under the new town hall or *Rathaus*. It was quite an experience to go there with him. Although food coupons were the first requirement of even an indifferent meal, this student, after a whispered conversation with the waiter, would disappear into the kitchens.

His disappearance and subsequent re-appearances were made as unobtrusive as possible, as was our seating arrangement, in order not to arouse the curiosity of the not so fortunately acquainted guests. The subsequent meals served, which to our unaccustomed eyes looked more lavish than they really were, were a delight: sometimes a few slices of meat, an egg or two, or little sausages, rolls and, on one occasion a small portion of real butter, that rare commodity of which infants received a small ration on their ration cards, teenagers a slightly larger allocation, while all adults were restricted to margarine. And it behoved one not to look too closely at that either, for the green streaks in its vivid yellow looked neither appetising nor healthy.

This producing of meals without coupons proved, as is usually the case, that it is who one knows that counts.

On one occasion, and a day to remember, a waiter appeared after the meal and put something down, hidden beneath a serviette, and wonder of wonders I found two very small chocolates wrapped in tissue; and another time I was given a small bottle of apricot brandy to take home.

These treats, however, only occurred during the first year of the war and were undoubtedly the result of much hoarding in advance, for there were no such commodities on the market on a retail level. The production of luxuries stopped on the first day of war.

Such evenings were the only ones in which I forgot, for a short time, the loneliness and desolation of being separated so completely from my loved ones.

Other outings, however, were not so pleasant. One I remember in particular was at the Café Drei Könige (Three Kings). Four people and I, one of them in uniform, sat down after the evening's lessons were over and were chatting quietly amongst ourselves while we drank 'coffee'. The tables were relatively close together and a zealous citizen must have noticed my accent. Suddenly there was uproar. He insisted to all and sundry that I must be a spy. My first instinct was to rush away from the place, but one of the boys with me kept his head. Quietly he told the man that if necessary my passport would be produced to a police officer and no one else. Minutes were like hours before the obnoxious, attention-seeking man finished his own coffee and left, but those with me insisted that we stay seated until he did so. I vowed never to go into that café again.

For the first few months of war, dancing was still permitted. The small *Lokale* (or dance clubs) in Leipzig, with their revolving dance floors set in the middle of the very small rooms, where one could have a quiet drink and dance, or relax, were a novelty to me; as were the dances in the open air on conveniently placed board flooring, surrounded by lawns, gardens and trees in the grounds of suburban inns. Gradually, however, it became apparent that there was more freedom of movement on these floors, resulting from a dwindling clientele as the men were enlisted.

Unfortunately these places were no escape from the eye of the law for a feature of these dances was the ever-present individual with steely eyes and stern demeanour, always ready to tap the too 'daring' dancer on the shoulder and order 'Jazz *verboten*'. I doubt if those persons actually knew what jazz was, but it seemed to me that the slightest movement other than that of tiny shuffling steps was classed as 'jazz'. It would have been amusing to see the reaction of one of these men to the Twist or Frug.

Eventually, the fighting as it escalated put even these recreations on the long list of *verboten* activities, and anyone who wished to dance had to do so illicitly behind closed doors. With this last restriction, all visible signs of gaiety ended. There was nothing more left. Just the everyday round of existence.

The youth of Germany became, overnight, sober citizens, not by choice or years of knowledge, but by law. The *Weinstuben*, though, where students went to drink, were filled to capacity. Even there, however, there was forced laughter, hard laughter and squealing voices, but no joy. Most of these places were also forbidden to the military, although now and again a soldier slipped in, his uniform hidden under a civilian coat, as he sought a few minutes' forgetfulness with a bottle of Greek wine; risking, of course, the consequences of being picked up by the frequent patrols which from time to time checked such taverns.

Apart from a very few soldiers, either recently enlisted and in nearby barracks or on leave from the front, the clientele became younger and younger as the ever open maw of the Army gradually swallowed up those considered old enough to hold a gun. Yet those still left, sang the old songs, '*Gloriamus Igitur*' and others, to the accompaniment of beer mugs pounded on tables scored with carvings of past generations. A fascination for me was to watch the bartenders chop radishes of the large white variety. Holding the pungent vegetable with one hand they swiftly chopped with huge butcher's knives, and miraculously the radish would turn into a concertina with paper-thin leaves. Then a thumb and forefinger was plunged into salt and this was rippled evenly along the radish.

It was a hard life for young people, lack of entertainment, often resulting in mischief, but all paths led in the same direction eventually. Boys of seventeen and eighteen were caught up by a giant uniformed fist and put down in the ranks, and girls of the same age pressed into service in the factories. There was only one important thing in those days – the Army and its maintenance.

4

My apartment was about twenty minutes by tram from the centre of Leipzig, where the school was situated, and after a few months I had the opportunity of moving closer, into a *pension* where food was included.

This *pension* was in a most imposing building, Nietzsche's Märchenhaus (Fairy-tale House). This was where the famous philosopher Friedrich Nietzsche once lived and was located on Thomasius Street. About six storeys high, the façade was elaborately carved in relief with tiny fairy-tale figures, trees and flowers. It was close to the Thomas Church, where, at the beginning of the eighteenth century, the great composer Johann Sebastian Bach was the organist and choirmaster.

I visited this church, famous through the ages for its choir school and choir. Climbing the steep stair to the gallery, I'd sit and listen to the lovely music. I have a shrewd guess that, if it were possible for a person's thoughts to be superimposed in some manner on his or her environment, the stained glass window opposite the seat I always occupied must be covered with mine; the hopes, memories, longings, all those things a lonely person thinks of.

It was no unusual thing, when I looked down on the congregation, to get glimpses of jackboots or a black uniform half-hidden beneath a long civilian overcoat. There may have been many of the SS troops who had turned against religion or perhaps were afraid to acknowledge their belief, but there were also many who held onto it and contrived to practise it against all odds.

When reading propaganda, the word 'majority' certainly did not mean *all*, and quite often may not have meant even half, but newspapers during wartime (and certainly in these more recent times of so-called peace) grossly exaggerate, leading to a whole nation being judged by a minority.

Outside Germany, it was said at this time that the country had turned its back on its churches. More likely the real reason was that every person belonging to either the Catholic or the Evangelist or Lutheran churches were forced to pay church tax, which was deductible from salaries at source. Thus people opted officially to leave their religions in order to save the tax, which was, in any case, being diverted to other coffers than those of the churches concerned.

I belonged to the Church of England, and while it was considered to be equivalent to the Lutheran Church, there was no space provided for it on the wage slips, so I was exempted from the tax.

Changing one's address was controlled by the Government and endorsed by the police. This entailed completing endless forms which had be presented to the police office of the district in which the new address was situated. In Germany one could not just *move*. To do so was a major operation, not only involving sorting, discarding and packing, but also the research necessary for the answering of countless questions, some pertinent, some, I am afraid, not so pertinent. Be it noted that the expression 'moonlight flit', as applied in England to those moving overnight to unknown destinations to avoid paying bills, could not be translated here. This was a land of signing and paying on the dotted line. Here was *order*.

On the day of my move, it was pouring with rain and just by chance, another tenant was moving into the *pension* on the same day. This person offered to take my completed forms to the police, together with hers. However, this time the police were not as amicable as I had found them at headquarters.

'England can come herself!' snapped the official in charge, throwing my despised papers back onto the counter. They were regretfully returned to me about an hour later and 'England' donned a raincoat, unfurled her umbrella and marched, in none too good a mood, through the rain, to the police station.

By the time I got there I was soaked and very irate. All

caution thrown to the winds, I placed the form on the counter and waited. I had expected some nasty remarks, but to my surprise the officer picked up the form, nodded to me and turned back to his files. I still waited.

He looked up.

'Well?' I said.

'Well, what?' His face registered no interest.

My face flushed with anger, for apparently I had been made to attend just out of spite.

'I think,' I blurted out, 'that you had better take a good look at England's head, there are no more horns sticking out of it than of your own.' With that I stormed out.

Frankly, as the rain cooled me off, I was afraid that my temper had taken me too far. Would there be repercussions for my insolence? Or was the official just bewildered at my stupid remarks? Or, even, was my German so bad that it had not been understood? Perhaps it wasn't even he who had turned the papers back in the first place.

But no. A Might greater than any Government on this earth was protecting me from my own folly.

The *pension* to which I moved was situated on the third floor of the Fairy-tale House and reached by a lift. It was run by a most extraordinary character, named Frau Aggarwal. This woman could have been anything from forty to sixty years of age. Ugly, rather grubby, and practically blind, she had a most beautiful daughter, aged ten, named Shakuntala.

Frau Aggarwal told us that she had met an Indian student in Germany, married him and gone to India, believing herself to be his only wife, only to discover another three wives already there when she arrived. I think she probably meant another wife and two live-ins.

She had made the best of a bad job, and in due course gave birth to this daughter, who clearly showed her Indian parentage in her flowing black hair, dark skin and dark liquid eyes.

When the child was two years old the mother began losing her eyesight, the loss, she said, being precipitated by the strong sunlight. This was the reason, or so she said, for her return to

Germany; minus her husband, but richer for her beautiful daughter.

The advantages of being in this *pension* were that it was near the school and I got regular meals. These were not cooked as hygienically as one would have desired and there were only too often matchsticks in the food, dropped there by Frau Aggarwall's fumbling blindness. Between her chain-smoking and the matches used for lighting the gas, there were plenty of them; however, the actual food was definitely better than the eternal potatoes and tomatoes and thin soup on which I had been existing.

As for the matchsticks, these soon became a source of competition between the residents; a competition conducted in silence, for we had no wish to antagonise our landlady. The winner, or loser, by whichever standard one chose to classify the results, was indicated by the number of wooden sticks bristling around the edge of a plate and pointed out by a quietly indicative finger.

One of the residents was a young married woman named Gretl Wormland. Her husband, who was stationed in a nearby barracks, sometimes came to dine with us and Fritz seemed to have the aptitude of a retriever for scenting out these doubtful wooden delicacies from his dinner plate.

There were other tenants in the *pension*. One was a female dentist and her small son (where her husband could be we had no idea, for he was certainly never mentioned). There was also a spinster, ugly and of enormous proportions, who spent all her time answering and putting advertisements into the marriage columns of the newspapers. This, naturally, gave rise to open speculation among the other tenants; although to our knowledge she never met with success. The other room changed tenants so often while I was there that I lost count.

About this time I was approached by the *Wahlamt*, an office concerned with naturalisation. I was informed that because my father had been born in Germany, I was, according to German law, a German citizen. This I denied, as I had done earlier to the police, I had, I insisted, been born in England and owned a British passport. There was a difference in the laws of the two countries. According to German law a child took its father's nationality. I stressed that in England one took the nationality of one's land of birth. I also knew that my father had never registered my birth at the German Embassy in London, and I had my British passport to support my claim.

The *Wahlamt* couldn't prove that my father had registered at the Embassy and I couldn't prove he hadn't, and chance in the form of hostilities was on my side for a change ... at least I thought it was.

I knew that my father should have returned to Germany to serve in the Kaiser's Army in 1905, but had failed to do so, preferring to remain in England because he had met my mother in that year, and intended to marry her and adopt her country as his own. Between 1905 and 1911 he received three orders to return to Germany, all of which he had ignored and finally in 1911 he had been posted in Germany as a 'Military wanted' and in England as 'Stateless'.

I had no intention of going into such detail with the *Wahlamt*, which was obviously out to prove my German nationality by hook or by crook. I felt that the less I told them the better and, apart from this, my German, while rapidly becoming more fluent, was hardly capable of coping with lawyers and legalities.

Suddenly, to my surprise, the argument was abandoned and I was left in apparent peace. I guessed that my correspondence was being controlled, and as further proof, if that were needed, there came a day when I was sent for by the Gestapo.

The building occupied by this governmental section was not imposing outside, nor did it give any indication of the sinister interior. The path from its wicket gate was covered by a rose-arbour. However, the clang with which a metal inner door closed behind me was not conducive to a particularly secure feeling for an ordered visitor.

Standing inside were the usual complement of jackbooted, stern-faced officials and the overused mode of greeting was continually being exchanged.

'*Heil Hitler!*' The heels clicked.

'*Heil Hitler!*' I answered, this time being careful that no inflexions of voice crept into my reply which could be mis-interpreted. I wondered if there were individuals still daring somewhere in this land of the swastika to use the outmoded but amiable and pleasant sounding '*Grüss Gott!*' or even '*Guten Tag!*'

When I had first gone to Germany, my cousin Fritz, with whose sister I had lived for a short time prior to the war (the son and daughter of my father's sister, Anna), had a friend, a Peter Loebel, who had been in the SA (the National Socialist *Sturmabteilung* – the political section of the SS, or Storm Troopers). Peter had asked me to teach him English.

About a month before hostilities commenced he arrived for his lesson looking pale and worried. The Gestapo, during their detailed and involved investigations into the backgrounds of citizens and their antecedents, had ferreted out that Peter's great-grandmother had been a Jewess. Until now, Peter had, himself, been ignorant of the fact and now he said there would be no option for him other than to leave the country if he could. At that time, fresh from England, where nothing so dramatic as this ever happened, at least to my knowledge, I thought he was romancing and dismissed the conversation from my mind as sheer fantasy.

We had always met for the English lessons at Gasthaus zur Schwalbe, a good mile away from where I was living, on a country road past Sachs Park (an estate closely associated with the musical Sachs family and where the soprano Erna Sachs still lived). This road was little used during the week. Our reason for choosing this secluded spot was that it was very quiet on weekdays and consequently suitable for studying. Most of the trade in the Gasthaus was done on Sundays when folk took their Sunday walks, with this inn as a stop-off for coffee and cake.

I usually walked out to it in the daylight and was very glad of Peter's company on the return journey, for I had always been rather afraid of the dark, and the tall gloomy trees lining the road held all kinds of imaginary horrors for me.

There came the day when I sat in my usual seat at the inn and waited, but Peter didn't come.

'Well, *Fräulein*, your friend hasn't arrived today,' said the over-fat landlady.

'No. I expect he was detained.'

She looked at me very queerly, but I was far too worried, thinking about the creepy return journey in the dark to care what was on her mind. She may have thought that we met because we were in love and that I had been jilted; but I now think that it was more than likely she had been questioned about our meetings, for the innocent and normal gatherings of two or more in those days were open to interrogation of one kind or another.

None the less, I had to get home and I paid my bill and left. Coming out onto the road, I crossed it and slowly started the long walk home; but once out of sight of the inn, I quickened my pace. My feet raced. I ran and ran as if the devil himself were behind me. Not until I reached the edge of the suburb where I lived with my cousins did I slow down and begin to think again of Peter.

My first thought was to telephone his landlady.

I slipped into the nearest telephone booth and dialled his number. 'Hello! Is Peter Loebel there?' I asked.

'*Nein!* There's no Peter Loebel here,' an impatient female voice answered.

'But he lodges there, doesn't he?'

'*Ja! Ja!* But two days ago he packed and left in a hurry. Who knows the reason? Paid me up and left. Just like that.'

'Did he say he would be back? Did he leave a message?' I was thinking more about my books which he still had in his possession than of him.

'No message...' and with that the receiver at the other end slammed onto its hook.

That was the last I had heard of him until I received a letter written from Belgium. I recognised his writing, but he hadn't signed it.

This was the letter which had been intercepted by the Gestapo and had led to my summons to their headquarters in Leipzig.

Now, as I stood before a black-uniformed member of the

40

Party, I was frightened. Question followed question, all of which I answered to the best of my ability. There was little sense in holding anything back and there was no reason to do so. In any case, I was so scared that I couldn't have made a good job of ad libbing a fabrication. My best bet was to acknowledge the reason for a sketchy acquaintanceship and stick to my guns that I had no idea of his background.

Finally my questioner pushed back his chair, crossed the room, and held a whispered conversation with another individual, who to this moment had remained silent. From time to time he turned and looked at me, and I wondered what would happen. I trembled and waited.

A suitable period having elapsed ... sufficient perhaps in their opinion to bring me to an acquiescent frame of mind, my interrogator returned to his desk.

'Now, *Fräulein*! We have to be quite sure what is going on.' He took a clean sheet of paper and a pen and placed them before me.

'You will write to this Loebel, a nice friendly letter asking him where he is and what he is doing, and add that it is quite safe for him to sign the letter. It's no concern of yours, *Fräulein*. All you are concerned with is to do as you are told.'

Dear God! This was stark reality. Drama had become fact. Here I was, sitting behind locked doors, helpless as a puppet on a string, and I was fully aware I had no alternative but to make the movements generated by the strings these men were operating.

I wrote.

After I had written the letter I was dismissed. The iron door opened. I was again in the sunshine, but I would never be the same person; I had become older, and hopefully much wiser. Certainly more thoughtful. The young, carefree girl was disappearing fast. She had of necessity to disappear. This was no place for frivolities. This was stern, stark life. To exist one had to be on guard day and night.

A few weeks later I received another letter, this time signed 'Peter'. It was patently obvious, even to my untrained eye, that I was not the first to read it. I could see nothing subversive in it, and apparently whoever read it first had also discounted its importance, at least as far as I was concerned. The incident was, I hoped, closed, and I felt relieved not to have to make another trip to that frightening place.

But that was the last communication I had from him and I didn't answer it.

In the summer of 1940 I asked permission of the police to leave Leipzig during my two-week vacation from the school. As usual, I was short of cash and so decided to take a train to Saalfeld in Thüringia, which was not too far distant, and to walk from there in the peace of the countryside, staying the first two nights at a village along the way. I had been to Saalfeld before, in 1938, while staying with my aunt Martha in Gera, and the place intrigued me.

It lay about forty-five miles southwest of Gera on the northern edge of the Thüringian forest. Deep down under the hillside are grottos and caves known as the Hubertushöhle. These caves contained mineral springs, and tours were available, or rather had been available, through electrically lit paths, and the stalagmites and stalactites presented a fairytale picture with exceptionally lovely colourings.

The first night I stayed at one of the picturesque old inns in the town. Saalfeld was first mentioned in documents as early as 899 as a royal palace, but the present town dated from 1200 and a Benedictine monastery was established there in 1704. When I was there, the town had some beautiful medieval buildings still in a state of good preservation, but the caves were closed.

The next day I set out with a rucksack on my back and wandered through the woods until I came to a tiny village, the name of which I have long since forgotten. Here, at least, there was no outward sign of war. Quiet prevailed in the drowsy sunshine and the only social life appeared to be that of the old men who sat on a circular bench round the base of a huge shady tree, talking of old times, or sometimes not talking but just puffing on their well-matured pipes.

The only room available was a tiny one set in the eaves of the village guesthouse. This was clean and adequate. It didn't take long to get acquainted with a few of the other guests and one of them, a young girl from Siemenstadt in Berlin, whose name I also cannot remember, joined me in my daily walks. The time passed very pleasantly.

We walked one day to Schwarzetal, a deeply wooded valley. Rising from its centre was sugarloaf-shaped hill, topped by a *Schloss*. Again there were no outward signs of war and it was not until much later, in fact a good time after the war, that I learned the reason for a most official-looking barricade on a little path leading up to it: the King of the Belgians was imprisoned there. But we two girls forgot world affairs for a time and happily and lightheartedly scrambled over the rocks; sat under trees; and, at one point when our feet got tired and hot with walking, clambered out into the middle of a stream under a waterfall and dangled our bare feet in the icy water which splashed from above.

I am sure that in the darkest and most depressing times we are granted flashes of beauty to refresh us and strengthen us for whatever trials may be ahead. This was one of them.

Another day we went blueberry picking. About eight of us set out together and we stooped over the low bushes glutted with fruit. We were soon well on the way to filling our baskets. Suddenly as I put my hand into a bush for a handful of berries, an adder reared its head. I have a horror of anything creeping, even worms are enough to send shivers down my spine and, as far as snakes are concerned, I am no heroine.

I ran. I ran so hard and so fast that I was prepared to agree with my companions when they laughed at my expense. According to them, and this was probably no exaggeration, they said I ran for about a mile without stopping.

At this point one of the group caught up with me and calming my shuddering said, 'Come along back. They have killed it, it's harmless now.'

I walked back; but, on arriving at my starting point, someone held the dead reptile hanging limply from a stick towards me.

'There now ... see ... Dead!'

43

They said that I ran away again for another mile until I could be stopped. Maybe it was true – the laugh was on me.

However, snakes apart, these heavenly two weeks were to be the last near carefree ones for many years. Soon after, the mutterings of war penetrated to even the most hidden and secluded parts of the country and its ugliness left its mark in practically every family.

5

One day, two young men registered with the Berlitz School. Carl Baun and Fritz Meyer were both from Steisslingen, a little village close to the borders of Switzerland in the neighbourhood of Schaffhausen.

They said they wished to study English and they each paid for one hundred lessons, which was most unusual. No one thought at the time it was strange they had come such a very long way for tuition – even though there were Berlitz schools much nearer to their home.

The lessons began, but neither of the boys was adept at learning any language and I doubted they would achieve the purpose for which they had come; nor could I figure out that purpose as it didn't appear they intended following any foreign language employment, which would have been impossible anyway as they were both near the 'calling-up' age.

Carl was nineteen, of medium height, black-haired and brown-eyed. A pleasant, although rather irresponsible fellow, he was always smiling.

His friend Fritz was of smaller build, quieter and not so outgoing.

It wasn't long before Carl invited me to go out with him for a cup of coffee. There was nothing unusual about this. Quite often a pupil or pupils taking the last lesson of the day went for coffee with the teachers before going home.

Fritz always accompanied us. Coffee and cake (the latter as long as the coupons lasted) ... that was about the sum total of entertainment these days. We visited all the cafés in turn: The Eden, Corso, Hochhaus, Naschmarkt, Schwarz, Reginabar, Intimebar and Perner. On rare occasions we left the more intimate and cosy atmosphere of these one-time dance bars and tried the more 'select' company at the Panarama ... but this was a rather stuffy place for young people, and its conservative orchestra was not so pleasing to me as the zither to be heard in some of the other cafés.

I think it very probable that under normal circumstances I would have had no interest in these boys nearly eight years my junior, but there are more ways than one to form a friendship leading to romance. Some develop on the rebound; some from an unhappy love affair; some from boredom, and, in my case, probably it was an escape route from loneliness, from a need of protection or from a fear of the daily problems of existence ... that is, just plain *company*.

Christmas was not too far off and one day Carl said that his mother had written from Steisslingen and would like me to spend Christmas with them there, as she felt that I must be very lonely. I think it more probable that Carl had written asking her to invite me.

I also knew that those special days would be terribly lonely if I spent them in Leipzig with only thoughts of my parents to keep me company. The prospect of seeing something new and meeting new people was a very pleasant one. For one thing, I would see something more of the German countryside.

Of course, permission had again to be obtained from the police department for me to leave Leipzig, even for a few days, but this was more readily granted than I could have anticipated and the three of us left in a holiday mood.

It was an exceptionally long and drawn-out journey through the black-out. The unlighted train and the stations through which it passed intensified the biting wind and swirling snow outside the windows. At one station, Weissenfels, we had to change trains.

It was bitterly cold on the platform and the small waiting room was packed with people, many of whom were sitting on the floor. Even this was an enviable position, for in spite of the fact that there was no fire in the minute fire-grate provided for heat in pre-war days, the heat from the many people crowded together was something to be envied by those who could not squeeze their way in and had to remain outside.

Enquiries as to when the train for Stuttgart would arrive brought little comfort, for schedules could be disrupted at any time.

To keep blood circulation going we had to keep on the move, stamping our feet up and down the platform, and curbing our impatience as best we could until at last the train steamed into the station.

Then, it was every man for himself. No one got off the train, which was already packed. Those intent on boarding it used the doors and even the windows, and it always strikes me as incongruous that no one found it amusing when a fat woman was being heaved through a window, long woollen underwear showing beneath dragged-up skirts, and overly thick calves waving violently, as she was pulled to the interior of the railway coach. There was no humour in such a situation, just urgency, and envy that, no matter how she had achieved it, she was aboard.

We managed to force our way onto the train and found that the coaches were dimly lighted. Before departing, the guard saw to it that all windows were again closed and all the blinds completely drawn down, thus precluding even the reflected white of the snow. The result was that the countenances of the passengers were ghostlike; when aeroplanes flew overhead, heard but not seen, the eeriness intensified, for then the scant lighting inside the coaches was snuffed out and we swept along in total darkness.

Government orders were that should enemy aircraft be flying in the vicinity, trains were to continue without stopping until reaching a terminus, and we felt like sitting ducks waiting for something to hit us.

It took twenty-three hours to reach Stuttgart; immediately the train reached that terminus, we were bundled out and herded in double-quick tempo to the station cellars. There we crouched and listened to the thud of bombs and wondered just how bomb-proof the cellars were. Eventually we were released by the all-clear hooter and emerged to complete our journey without mishap.

At the small town of Singen, near the Swiss frontier, we

were lucky enough to catch the one daily bus for the nine-mile drive to Steisslingen. The road led for one and one half miles to a junction, where it branched. The right road led to Constance and Radolfzell and the left road to our destination on the Stockach road.

It was like travelling through fairyland for me. Black forests converged on the road from each side to end in deep snow-banks thrown up by the snowploughs. The trees all wore thick white cardigans of snow which as the bus brushed by, fell off with a ploppy sound.

The house where Carl lived with his mother was owned by his grandparents, Xaveria and Johann Fuchs, who lived on the upper floor.

It was a typical farmhouse for those parts. To the left of the front door there was a parlour kept for guests and special occasions. It had a highly polished wood floor, as opposed to most of the houses, where the raw wood floors were kept strewn with rushes or straw, and this applied even to those occupied by some of the more wealthy farmers. I soon discovered that the occupants of this house considered themselves somewhat better than their neighbours. Leading from the parlour was Carl's mother's bedroom. At the end of the front passage was the kitchen, opening onto an open, boarded verandah with a lavatory at one end and a high wood storage area at the other – walled off from the barn which backed onto it. Steps led to a square yard.

On the other side of the front door was the stable and cow-house, to which access could be gained not only from outside, but from the front passage in the house itself. Upstairs, leading off a small landing, was another bedroom opening onto a wooden verandah, and on this was another toilet at one end. Here one could sit and survey the far-flung view over the fields and hills and, if socially inclined, wave to a passing neighbour! There was no privacy, nor was any sought, there being no door to this primitive convenience.

I was amused, though, to notice that a hole in the wall had been blocked most efficiently with a picture of Hitler. A picture of this 'gentleman' was a *must* in all homes, and it says much for the daring of these farmers in the south, that while complying with the requirements, they had the audacity to use it so practically. I might add that Adolf hung upside down, a finesse of Carl's grandfather. Let it be said that the Führer made an excellent draught excluder in this not exalted position.

Over the parlour was another huge room, in this case used for drying herbs picked painstakingly by Carl's grandmother, and with very little furniture beyond a table and a chair. Behind this was the bedroom occupied by the old couple.

Over the cowshed and extending out back was the barn. I found that the cosy proximity of hay and grain to the house was the reason for the squeaking and rustling of mice in the walls and, on the odd occasion, the pattering of tiny feet across the feather quilt in the night. An added attraction to the rodent family was the great smoked hams and sides of bacon and sausages hanging from the rafters of upstairs bedrooms, for while they were inaccessible to the sharp teeth, they filled the rooms with strong, heady and attractive aromas.

I was introduced to Carl's grandparents. His grandmother was tiny and the wiriest little person I had ever seen. Her long black skirts reached down to her ankles in the fashion of all women, whether young or old, in that district of peasants. Even the gayest young girl used to the prettiest of dirndls, in accordance with custom and after the doubtful glory of usually a black wedding dress and white veil, was condemned to this drab garb. Immediately following the ceremony they donned long black skirts, thick black stockings, black boots, a tucked-in high-necked blouse and the inevitable black apron. Young girls were swept away on the tide of matrimony and were transformed into hardworking housewives and farmhands. The odd exceptions were looked upon as trollops and lazy good-for-nothings, but custom being custom, there were few such rebels and the majority seemed resigned, although not jubilant, with their lot.

I always felt that grandmother Xaveria rather despised being married to a farmer, even to one of such standing as her husband, for she managed to include the statement 'I am a

49

Hertenstein' pretty freely in her conversations. However, I never found out who the Hertensteins had been, or were, and she never enlightened me.

Grandfather Johann Fuchs had a bristling moustache. Very tall, kindly, he was not an overly intelligent man, but of stubborn stock, born of the soil, knowing only work and the fields all his life.

Their two children still living (one had been killed in the First World War) were both married. Johann, who lived with his wife and two sons, Roderick and Heribert, at an inn, Gasthaus zur Trauben, and Anna, Carl's mother, who was now married to a man named Repp and had been divorced some years earlier from Carl's father, Eugen Baun. Repp's Christian name escapes me; I rarely saw him and on those occasions he was known as 'Vati' to us, the childish shortening of 'father'.

I always felt that grandfather Fuchs was not entirely happy with his daughter's present marriage. He never seemed comfortable in the presence of Vati Repp. This could possibly have been a matter of religion. Grandfather Fuchs and his family were Roman Catholic, as were almost all of the residents of the village. He would, therefore, not readily be reconciled to the divorce and remarriage of his daughter. Again, it might have been because, as I found out later, Vati was involved with the Communist party, or perhaps it was just that grandfather, being a soft-hearted and kind man, could not understand the hardness of the other man's character.

Grandfather was too old to understand much about politics and too uncomplicated to take the trouble to hide his hate of Hitler and his regime. We often had near brushes with authority when he expressed himself too freely on the subject. While in his hate of the regime his opinions were the same as those of Vati, there was complete difference in application, and for completely opposing reasons.

Grandfather's very simplicity had its humorous side and I well remember the day he led his oxcart from a sideroad onto the village main street, grandmother perched on the top of the load, when a military vehicle whizzed by, narrowly missing the cart. The old lady, afraid she was going to be toppled over, gave a scream, only to be told, 'Stay where you are! Stay where you are, Xaveria, we are insured.' He never saw the humour of his remark, for on perceiving that the car had been occupied by uniformed officials, he burst in to a stream of invectives against the Government.

My language difficulties had ironed themselves out by now; but, here in the southern part of Germany, it was like listening to a completely new tongue. The dialect was so different. Slowly, however, my ear became schooled to the inflections and gradually I picked up the idiomatic phrases, of which there were many.

Here, too, I discovered that even in this day and age, under the same iron government, the village folk still used the greetings '*Grüss Gott*' and '*Fuhr Di Gott*' (God go with you), it was a very pleasant relief from the harsh forced greeting of the towns and cities.

It was a lovely Christmas – like nothing I had ever seen as far as the scenery was concerned, deep snow everywhere, the pine trees were laden with it. In the early mornings, only a few yards from the last houses on the village outskirts, the spoor of small deer could be seen crisscrossed in all directions, the cold having driven them closer than usual to human habitation.

A few hundred feet from the house, in a saucer-like depression in the land, was an ice-covered lake on which children skated. On one side, leading down from the country road to the lakeshore was a cider apple orchard, the bare black branches of the trees promising beauty in the spring. A pine forest rose from a hill on the opposite shore. If one stood on the lakeshore and looked up over the orchard, one could see, lonely by the roadside, a wayside cross. These crosses were frequent in this part of the Catholic district but this particular one was, for me, exceptionally beautiful, for each time I saw it, it seemed to reinforce my sometimes weakening courage.

The village was pretty too. Two main streets ran at right angles to one another. One was the main Stockach to Singen road and the other just a wide village street leading for about a quarter of a mile or so to where it petered out into the

51

forest. The last house on it was the forester's house. The church, tiny and extremely pretty, stood on a hill in the centre of the village.

It is difficult to determine now what my emotions truly were at this time. I thought I loved Carl, but now, looking back, I am certain that it was a falsely translated sense of extreme loneliness. I was so desperately alone that even my own loves and hates were playing me false. I wanted to be with him, to know that I belonged, because there was no one else. Anyone who had seemed kind would have fitted the bill equally well. I was in the position of a person bearing an enormous load too heavy to carry alone and waiting to pass it on to the first one who offered.

Yet my sense of right and wrong, my instincts, still forced me to hesitate and, when Carl asked me to marry him, I found I could not answer immediately. I told him to think it over very well because he was so much younger than I, there being eight years' difference in our ages.

He was not to be put off, though, and continued his efforts to persuade me. Little did I know then that he was under extreme pressure to bring about the marriage, from the Government.

When the short holiday came to an end, we both returned to Leipzig, I to teach and he to learn. I find it significant now, but did not realise its importance then, that Fritz Meyer did not return with us. I asked him why and he said he was needed at home around the farm; that he was no longer interested in learning English and that he would be called up soon. His parents and Carl gave me the same reasons. Certainly he did not fill the need at home for long and I doubt if he had ever had an interest in learning a language beyond the possibility that it might keep him from the trenches a few months longer.

It was only a short time later that Herr and Frau Meyer said goodbye to their uniformed son, as he joined the ranks, like so many thousands of other young men, for the short training periods before they were sent to the front.

My life in Leipzig went on as before, but Carl took a position in a florist's shop, Hanisch, during the day. I never had time to discover what his duties were but he told me that this was the only position he could get in view of the fact that, because of his age, he would soon be called up. As a consequence any employment could only be of a temporary nature. This job lasted only three weeks and then he said he had obtained work in a factory not too far from where I was living.

But suddenly, by some uncanny instinct, I felt something was wrong. I can remember quite distinctly when the suspicion entered my mind. For no reason at all, as I was walking to work and with no thought other than that he also had gone to work at six thirty in the morning from his lodgings or that I would see him in the school in the evening, it was almost as if a light had been switched on in my mind. I had no cause to doubt him, nothing led to this feeling, but with certainty I felt I had been told a lie.

Answering an impulse, I turned into the nearest telephone booth and rang the office where he told me he worked.

'Carl Baun? We have no one here of that name.'

'But you must have,' I insisted, and then asked for the foreman by name; for Carl had been explicit as to the names of those for whom he was working.

'There is no one by that name either, *Fräulein*,' a long-suffering voice drawled. I hung up.

That day seemed longer than any others, but eventually the hour for Carl's class arrived and he breezed in, his cheery grin the same as ever.

'Where have you been all day?'

'At work,' he said plumping himself down in the chair opposite me.

'I called you there, and they said they had never heard of you, nor of the foreman.'

'Oh! There was a misunderstanding.' He waved a deprecating hand. But now I had my doubts confirmed.

'Well, it's nothing to do with me, but it seems silly to say you are working if you are not, so what have you been doing all day?' I asked him again.

Suddenly his face crumpled, the grin disappeared. 'I have no job,' he said miserably.

'Well, what did you do? You didn't stay in your room all day did you?'

'No, my landlady thought I was working too. I sat in the waiting room at the *Hauptbahnhof* all day.'

I accepted this answer then, but now I wonder. It would be inevitable that most of my time with Carl would be spent wondering. This irresponsible being, whose every other word was to prove to be a lie, always gave plausible explanations for the lies when cornered; but were these explanations true, or were they lies as well? Did he lie because of a psychological condition or were tall tales forced upon him by officials, all forming part of the intrigue surrounding us both? Did he sit in the *Hauptbahnhof* each day? If not, what did he do? Was he, during those hours, before some Governmental committee arranging the trap into which I was to fall some day so neatly? I shall never know.

Not long after this I was sent for by the *Wahlamt* and was told that they could not prove me to be German against the evidence which I had produced, but that they understood I had an offer of marriage. There were veiled threats conveyed in this interview which could not be ignored, neither did they remain veiled for long.

The strings attached to the puppet again jerked and I was told to contact my parents for family papers. This request was sent through the governmental communiques. A letter from the Foreign Office to my father dated January 15, 1941 and a further letter dated February 13, clearly showed my father's refusal, rather than inability, to produce those papers.

The Under Secretary of State for Foreign Affairs presents his compliments to Mr Emil Shadlish and is directed by the Secretary of State to state that according to a report which has been received from the United States Consulate at Leipzig. Miss Alwine Joan Unwin Shadlish, a British subject residing at 26 Angerstrasse, Leipzig, called at that Consulate on the 23rd November 1940 and reported that she wished to marry a German citizen, Carl Baun of 51

54

Sidonienstrasse, Leipzig, who was born at Steisslingen, Bodensee on 25th October 1921.

2. Miss Shadlish stated that she wished to get married as soon as possible and requested that the following documents, which according to German law must be presented to the Bureau of Vital Statistics (Standesamt) before she can be married should be obtained from her parents, Mr and Mrs Emil Shadlish, 75, Cavendish Avenue, Harrow, Middlesex, namely certified copies of her parents' marriage certificate and her mother's birth certificate (she already possesses the birth certificate of her father).

3. If the documents in question are forwarded to the Foreign Office, the United States Embassy in London will be requested to endeavour to forward them to Miss Shadlish through the diplomatic channel, provided there is no objection.

FOREIGN OFFICE, S.W.1
15th January, 1941.

'The Under Secretary of State for Foreign Affairs presents his compliments to Mr Schaedlich and with reference to his letter of 22nd January 1941 is directed by the Secretary of State to inform him that it is not possible for the Foreign Office to request the United States Consul at Leipzig to take action in the sense desired.

If Mr Schaedlich will be good enough to inform the Foreign Office of the reasons for his inability to obtain the documents required by his daughter the United States Consul at Leipzig will be informed accordingly.

Should Mrs Schaedlich call at the Prisoners of War Department, Romney House, Marshall Street, S.W.1 between 9.30 a.m. and 5.30 p.m. she will be seen by a member of the staff.

FOREIGN OFFICE, S.W.1
13th February, 1941.

I must here explain the discrepancy in the spelling of our family name. The correct spelling is 'SCHAEDLICH' (a name with the curious English translation 'harmful'). My father had changed the spelling, through use, to 'Shadlish' for the simple reason that it was easier for people in England to write and to pronounce.

After they received this letter, the *Wahlamt* dropped the precedent and I was told the marriage would go through without any papers other than my birth certificate. This did not prevent the authorities, however, from insisting on the medical examination which took place before any marriage could be allowed.

6

In the meantime, Carl had been called to the forces and was quartered in the Prinz Wilhelm Barracks in Leipzig. He was called up in March 1941 and I well remember the day he had to report there for the first time. He had decided he would make a good impression and put on his best suit. The idea that anyone in the Army could be impressed was a big mistake. It was true. I was still not aware of the machinations of the service, but he had not been brought up under the same government as I, and should have known that smart or shabby, clean or dirty, lawyer or crossing-sweeper, having passed through the gates of a barracks, a man was a man and army material only: two arms, two legs, supplemented by a rifle ... and a number.

It was raining that first day as the new recruits, looking very young and defenceless, assembled on the barrack square waiting for the adventure to begin.

Several of us women, wives, mothers and girlfriends, had the temerity to go as far as the gates and from this vantage point watched through the railings. We didn't have to wait long.

Out strode an officer and with no more ado shouted ... *'HINLEGEN!'* (lie down).

The men looked at each other. One or two of the wiser ones flopped ungracefully to the muddy and pooled ground.

'HINLEGEN!' ... louder this time and with far more emphasis. With one accord the men sheepishly slid to the ground.

'AUFSTEHEN!' They stood.
'HINLEGEN!'
'AUFSTEHEN!'

This softening-up process went on, it seemed, for hours but probably lasted for fifteen minutes. Then there was a roar from the officer and the barrack guard moved towards the railings and ordered us to leave.

With one accord, we left. It was as simple as that.

Two days after this, I received a telephone call from Carl to go to the orderly office, where I was handed a parcel. It was Carl's civilian suit and other personal items considered to be unnecessary to barracks. His suit was filthy and still sodden We had learned too late that a bathing suit might have been more fitting for that first appearance.

It was six weeks before I saw him again. Recruits were not allowed from the barracks at all for that period of time. Even then their first outing was under the supervision of an NCO who took a detail of ten men at a time to some prearranged restaurant where they 'enjoyed' a muted and restrained freedom.

Carl managed to send out a note to me, which I received the morning of the day on which his particular 'Stube' was to be allowed out. It was very brief, only advising me of the time and the restaurant where they were going.

That evening, as soon as I was through at the school, I left and went to the restaurant. The noise of the laughter and loud talking guided one to their table. They were like children let out of school after the rigid enforcement of the past six weeks.

A chair was quickly pulled up for me beside Carl and we settled down to enjoy the brief time left.

It wasn't long, however, before the NCO in charge moved over and took the place of the man sitting on my other side. It is quite certain that a lot of the discipline was geared to subjection, and it was equally certain that this NCO was determined, not perhaps to cut Carl out, for I didn't think he had any interest in me as a person, but to make Carl feel uncomfortable through his attention to me.

Finally the NCO broke up the party with a swift order. The men sprang to attention, leaving me sitting facing a litter of empty beer glasses, coasters and cigarette ends. Swiftly the men turned and marched to the door and I rose and followed.

Carl, with the others, stared straight ahead and the order to march was given. The men in the group, still filled with a natural exuberance, motioned to me to step in with them. Without thinking I did so, and between them they moved me up slowly until I was next to Carl and we managed to talk a while under cover of the others singing their marching songs (they always sang when on the move).

Of course we hadn't gone unnoticed, how could I have been so silly as to think we would. After all, there were only ten men and the NCO and he was unlikely to stare straight ahead for long. When we arrived at the barracks, the NCO halted the men as the gate was opened from the inside. He then stepped back, beckoned to me and said loudly enough for Carl to hear, 'Wait here, *Schatzl* [sweetheart], and I'll be right out and we can spend the rest of the night enjoying ourselves.'

The men then disappeared into the barracks. I wasn't out to play Lily Marlene and took off as fast as my legs could carry me, boarded the first bus I could see, and got safely back to my room.

Carl told me afterwards that he had worried all night wondering what had happened and I suppose this was what had been in the NCO's mind.

After that outing, rules relaxed a little and twice a week Carl visited me for an hour each evening. It could have been longer but I was working at the school until 9 p.m. and he had to report back again by 10 p.m. Thus, all but a few minutes of our time was occupied, his with being turned into a military robot and mine with teaching.

One Friday evening in May 1942 at 5 o'clock I was summoned by the *Wahlamt* to present myself at the *Rathaus* at 11 o'clock the next morning. I was to be married to Carl. It was then that reality hit me – the trap was indeed closing. What I had deemed to be a friendship, and I'll admit a good friendship, was now serious.

In my case, since he had been called up, I had thought that the whole affair had been dropped, and, in spite of the form filling and medical examination, considered unimportant and not worthy of furtherance.

The phone call spurred me to action and I immediately boarded a streetcar and at the barracks was shown in to a Lieutenant Ludwig.

'Schütze Carl Baun! We are to be married tomorrow,' I stammered.

'So! I have heard already, I was advised this morning,' he said and laughed loudly. 'Well, well, little *Fräulein*, so you are to become a good German subject. I think we should celebrate by giving you a honeymoon. Let's see ... today is Friday ... shall we say he is to report back to the barracks on Monday morning?', and with that and a benevolent pat on the back, he left.

At nine o'clock that evening Carl arrived at my apartment. He only had a few minutes and we were deciding where to meet the next morning when there was a tremendous, ear-shattering crash outside my door.

We jumped up and rushed out. There on the floor was an enormous collection of bottles. Everywhere we looked there were bottles – big and little. Carl started to laugh and I could only wonder what was going on. I then saw Frau Aggarwal and several of the other residents were also laughing. 'It's your *Polterabend*,' one of them said. 'You have to have a *Polterabend* to bring good luck to your new life.'

Carl queried, 'But why *bottles*?' While they explained to me the practice of smashing old china and porcelain outside a door on the eve of a wedding, and to him that there was no china to be spared, only old bottles, I was wondering whether, because a superstitious event had been altered in that one respect, the marriage would be successful. However, it is doubtful if any such superstition, whether correctly carried out or not, could bring blessing on a union which was getting away to a governmentally forced start.

Carl returned to the barracks that evening and I remained in the solitude of my room, where I thought of what a wedding my parents would have planned for me and how it was to be now. I might add here that it was only after the end of the war that I found out that my father had refused to send the papers, for the request and denial had been solely between the German Government and the US Embassy.

On Saturday morning, May 17, 1942, Carl and I met and walked towards the *Rathaus*. I was wearing a black dress and a white hat, neither of them new. He wore his uniform. We might have been any couple on a shopping expedition.

There were few, if any, church weddings these days, and those performed before a priest must have taken place at odd hours, for they were neither mentioned nor seen. It is also possible that because clothes coupons met only the most stringent needs and often were inadequate even for those, that the ordinary clothes worn blended into everyday life. The traditional white satin and veil were impossible to buy in the stores even had the money and coupons been available.

Large gatherings of relatives and friends were also precluded because most of the men were away fighting and transportation from one place to another for civilians was at a minimum.

It is, therefore, inevitable that many young couples were united, snatching two or three days of leave, and some even taking advantage of a short 'stop-off' of one day, made possible by a soldier having to wait for a military train. They also took advantage of the swift and unceremonious civil proceedings in the town halls. Their vows, their clothes, the sparse scattering of women and old men attending each pair as witnesses, were drained of colour, vitality and joy. The pledge of matrimony had become a thing to be hastened; to be done with, no time for a gentle look or a quick smile.

The stone façade of the *Neues Rathaus* (new town hall) rose imposingly above us. A beautiful building outside, but inside it was a maze of offices used solely for civic matters. Brown-uniformed Party officials walked the corridors, seriously intent on their business. Here and there a black-uniformed member of the SS could be seen, and the only civilians stood, as we did, in a queue, waiting to be directed.

We were shown into a suite of rooms, and in the corridor outside a row of rather gloomy-looking couples waited to be called.

61

I had telephoned my cousin Hilda Lippman to come as a witness and so great was the fear of keeping the *Reich* waiting that she had come straight to the Town Hall without question. Although my aunt lived in Leipzig, we had little to do with one another as she disapproved of my father leaving Germany and of my being English, so it didn't occur to her to attend. Her passive dislike was to turn active before I was through.

Our other witness was a pupil from the Berlitz School, Hans Rolf, the only person I could find at such short notice who was over twenty-one and therefore qualified for such duty.

The room into which we had been ushered was a very large one with an enormous oil painting of Hitler, flanked by flags, which dominated one wall.

The registrar, sitting behind a large desk and eager only to get done with the long line of young men and women, barely glanced up from his desk until all the words had been spoken in proper order and the 'ceremony' concluded. Bewildered and scared, I wanted to get it over with and get away from the place. I wondered, too, whether all those waiting outside the room were 'normal' cases, with no complications such as ours; but they all seemed tense and I have no doubt each had, or would, bear their load of sorrow before long.

On the way to the Town Hall Carl and I had passed a florist's shop and on the spur of the moment he had bought me a bunch of narcissi and forget-me-nots. Those flowers were the only outward appearance of any untoward event, and I clutched them tightly as we were ushered outside again and another couple took our place.

Outside the door I was handed an enormous bouquet of flowers by an official from the *Wahlamt*. Presumably I had done well, in other words I had done what I was told to do. Another official handed us a large volume of *Mein Kampf*, which I never did get to read, nor wanted to; but it was useful as a storage place for used stamps, which I intended, if ever I did get home, to present to my stamp collector father. That wasn't to be, however, because fear at the end of hostilities was so great when the Russians entered Leipzig that my copy, with many another copy of Nazi literature, was thrown by my cousin into the river.

We returned to the *pension*, where Frau Aggarwal had made coffee for us and the 'wedding breakfast' was augmented by the arrival of Hans Rolf and another pupil, Ursula Herbst, who came to wish us well, bringing us cakes on which they had spent their valuable points.

The next morning I was sent for again by the *Wahlamt*. I obeyed.

'*Heil Hitler*,' an official greeted me. It occurs to me now how very flexible those two words were, since one could use them in so many ways.

'*Heil Hitler?* ... a query.

'*Heil ... Hitler*,' with lethargy, from those who had had enough, but who didn't know the mettle of the person being greeted.

'*HeilHitler*,' as an habitual greeting meaning nothing, or as a farewell, meaning even less than that. It could also be said with an inflexion of voice that made it sound like a rude statement.

This time my words were a query.

'You sent for me?'

'Your passport, please.'

'My passport? Why?'

'Never mind why. It has to be stamped with details of your marriage.'

I couldn't see why a British document should be stamped by the official of another country, but I was in no position to argue. I handed it over.

'Thank you! *Heil Hitler*,' he said taking it and turning away. This time there was no doubt as to the meaning. It was an official dismissal.

'Shall I wait for my passport?'

'You won't be needing it. You are a German subject,' he retorted, and disappeared with my treasured possession.

The next morning there was a knock on my door and I was faced with one of the active members of the Party, a woman I heartily disliked and who had looked down her nose at a 'foreigner' ever since I had first met her.

'There's a meeting on Tuesday evening for air attack defence – we shall be expecting you,' she announced.

For a moment I was silent, then I became angry. 'You mean I am required to know the procedure for protecting myself? I've always been precluded from such a meeting.'

'Yes, but now you are married to a German'.

Another result of my marriage was that I was now due to receive weekly support from the Army. Carl told me one day that I should go to an office near the Königsplatz to register for this 'perk' and he gave me explicit directions for finding the right room.

'Up to the second floor and on the right-hand side you will find room 212,' he said. 'There are three men in there dealing with military support and I have spoken to the white-haired one – he knows all about it.'

This proved to be another of his fairy tales – he had never been or spoken to any office in this regard. But I still hadn't realised how alert I had to be regarding any of his statements.

The next day in my lunch hour I followed the directions, climbed to the second floor, but was unable to find a room 212. An enquiry elicited the information that there was no such room. That evening, feeling I must have made a mistake, I went to the barracks and was allowed to speak to Carl. Again he gave me the directions. The next day again I could not find either the room or the man; but I did find a clerk who told me that only civil applications were dealt with in that building and that mine would have to be applied for at the barracks.

I faced Carl with this in the evening, and this time he told me he had telephoned someone else and that I should go to the barracks again the next day where the matter would be dealt with.

When I arrived I was so convinced that he was again lying that I asked the orderly if I could see him again. He directed me up the stairs, where I found Carl in a room. He took me to the window and pointing down to a building opposite said, 'You see that door, go through it and in the second room on the left you will find two officers who will deal with it.'

How I wanted to believe him, but by this time I was completely sceptical of everything he said, and becoming convinced that he had a lying complex. It was with some misgiving, therefore, that I left, and as I crossed the road I looked back to the window where he stood. He was nodding encouragingly, as I walked towards the building. I pushed open the door and went in to a short hall or corridor. There were only two doors leading from it, one of the left and one on the right. It was obvious that there was no such room. It had all been part and parcel of his lying sickness that I had been experiencing more and more frequently.

With a sinking feeling I knocked at the door on the left and told an officer behind the desk my errand. He looked grim, picked up the telephone, spoke to someone and only a few seconds later Carl entered and saluted. The officer took him severely to task and then ordered him from the room. When he had gone, the officer himself gave me proper instructions as to where to go to get the financial matter settled – and it wasn't the barracks.

A month after that, my husband was sent to the Russian front. All the past events had been dove-tailed by officialdom to make a pattern. Their objective had been achieved.

The few weeks we had been married were not happy ones. His lack of responsibility coupled with this propensity for lying gave me cause for grievous alarm. He never seemed able to speak a true word. It was definitely a disease.

He was given only a few hours to prepare for his departure although he did manage to telephone me and I boarded a tram to the barracks. We didn't see each other again for eighteen months.

None of the men knew their destination, but of course he said that he did, because they had been issued with light clothing, sunglasses, webbing belts etc. and that it would be Africa as their place of combat. He, of course, was very wrong. He was one of the unfortunate infantry men who marched into Russia through the bitter winter of 1941–42.

His diary, when I read it months later reiterated monotonously:

Marched 40 miles – dead tired – cold
Marched 28 miles – frozen feet
Tired – marched 60 miles
Marched ... marched ... marched...

Even so, he was one of the lucky ones during the winter. When he had been conscripted, he had been quartered in the same room with another young lad – Willi Knaust – whose father was a book publisher and local newspaper editor at Gräfenhainichen near Bitterfeld.

From Carl's diary I read that Willi had marched side by side with him day after day until his feet had started to blacken with frostbite. After a short rest during the advance, Willi had been unable to use his feet and had been abandoned in a ruined farmhouse where they had rested overnight.

After the news reached his parents, Herr Knaust wrote to me once or twice and I received one or two parcels from him containing writing paper, notebooks and luxuries such as the occasional roll of toilet paper.

Then that brief connection ceased too.

7

Carl had been gone some time when I realised that I should have to find other accommodation, for the *pension* where I was living would certainly be no place for a baby. My mother-in-law in Steisslingen was naturally delighted with the news and in one of her letters referred me to some acquaintance of hers in Leipzig who made toys. Even then she had no concern about how I would manage, as was to be the case for the rest of her life. Her only thoughts were of her grandsons and her son.

She suggested I visit these people and see if I could get hold of some toys for 'my grandson'. It seems a peculiar thing now to think of planning in such times for toys for a child not to be born for another six months; however, eventually the contact proved very useful.

I was on my way to see this man who made toys when an incident occurred which could have seemed amusing had it not had the potential for unpleasant consequences.

As I was walking near the Königsplatz with my mind on other things, I failed to observe a very strict regulation ... that it was strictly *verboten* to cross the centre of Königsplatz itself. One had to walk all around it; the walk was extremely long. I was well aware of the regulation so that there was no excuse for what I did and I was already in the middle of the forbidden area when a shout awoke me from my thoughts. A formidable policeman (during the war most German police-men were formidable and did not closely resemble the kind British 'bobbies' to whom I was accustomed) came stamping in my direction. I stopped.

'Where do you think you are going?'

From the corner of my eye I noticed a crowd gathering to

enjoy my discomfort. I don't think that people, at heart, enjoyed others' discomfort, but I do think it was such a relief for someone other than themselves to be in trouble; this in itself was the attraction.

I hesitated and then slowly stammered, '*Ich ver ... er ... Ich nicht ... ver...*'

I stopped and looked at him helplessly.

The officer got more and more red in the face and poured forth a torrent of German, which I understood perfectly Most of what he was saying was threatening and none of it was complimentary.

I gazed at him with a deepening look of puzzlement on my face and then said brightly, '*Ich ... English.*'

This did nothing to stop the flood of wrath he continued to pour over me, including this time details of the consequence of my shocking temerity. I again attempted a look of complete helplessness and said 'Er ... er...' and this must have achieved some success because all at once he stopped yelling, took a long look at me and waving a hand in disgust said in English, 'Oh ... go home.' He then stamped off.

I, in turn, scuttled off quickly on my errand to the toymaker before he could change his mind.

The business had been switched by the Government to the making of aeroplane parts. However, they still had a certain amount of stock in their apartment and from this I bought a large number of articles, all of them wooden pull-toys, trains, trucks and animals. These stood me in good stead later on, for each Christmas and birthday for both of my children until the end of the war. There would have been little else in their Christmas stockings otherwise.

In addition to these smaller toys, the man offered to sell me a rocking horse and a large and heavy bamboo swing. I was delighted to purchase them and felt that the financial outlay and the time I had to give to transporting these items across Leipzig was well spent.

In September it became imperative that I find other accommodation and the search could be put off no longer. To this end, I paid one of my very rare visits to my aunt on the

Herman-Meyerstrasse. She told me that a woman on the ground floor level occasionally let one of her rooms and I immediately contacted her.

The room available was extremely large, airy and light, located on a corner of the apartment complex. It was easy to heat with the big tiled oven standing by the door. It had two large windows and was ideal in that there was no objection to a baby.

Frau Lässig, my landlady, was a wiry little woman, always busy and never still. Determined and self-reliant, she ruled the roost in her family. Her husband, although a member of the Party, was a quite insignificant man in his own home. Their daughter Lotte, a girl of about twenty years who was no beauty, was generally regarded by all as being not quite right in the head.

An '*alte Kampfer*' (one of the original Hitler movement followers), Frau Lässig was a Nazi to her finger-tips. She told me that when her two children were small (she also had a married son), she had seen young men, idle, lounging on street corners, and when Hitler came into power and work was found for everyone, she felt that through him and the movement, her children would have a secure future.

To me she was always very good and did everything she could to protect and help me, in her own rough way. How she found time to do all her many acts of kindness, I shall never know.

Above all else, it was she who protected me from the unwelcome attentions of the Party; warning me when too great an interest was shown in my activities and insisting to the officials that she would give me the closest scrutiny and report anything suspicious. She cared for me as if I were her own daughter.

The day after I moved out of the Märchenhaus and into the room at Herman-Meyerstrasse, which was on the outskirts of Leipzig in the Kleinschocher district, the Märchenhaus was destroyed in an air raid.

8

Transportation in the city was, by now, reduced to the street-cars. Taxis were a thing of the past now and there were no privately owned cars. Indeed, prior to the war, there were very few of those and they were now useless because of lack of petrol for any machinery except that necessary to the war effort.

A week before my son, Michael Carl Unwin Baun, was born, my cousin, who had quite a walk to the nearest street-car route, went into labour ... a labour which promised to be short. The situation became so urgent that she finished up by being driven to the hospital on a fire engine.

Frau Lässig called my aunt, who lived in the apartment two storeys above where I had my room, and she, noting that my labour had begun, decided that history wasn't going to repeat itself.

My trip across Leipzig wasn't so spectacular as that of her daughter and it certainly wasn't pleasant. Two changes between streetcars and, it being early morning and rush hour for people going to work, it was standing room only and, need-less to say, no one offered me a seat.

After a difficult half-an-hour I arrived at the *Frauenklinik* and was hurried into what appeared to be a conveyor belt system.

In my ignorance of procedure I had no idea of anything con-nected with the birth of a child. What a difference to modern times when even the smallest child knows perhaps more than they should. So in my ignorance I had my hair set that week in order that I might give my baby a good first impression.

The nurses soon set me right in this regard. With no more ado, they parted my hair down the middle and plaited its shortness into two squiggles, which stood out on either side of my head, so that I looked like Topsy in *Uncle Tom's Cabin*. Not that I was in any shape to worry much about my appearance. A snowstorm raged outside and perhaps at that time, more than any other in my life, I felt alone. There was no one near me who cared if I lived or died, except clinically. My aunt was not interested in me beyond a wavering sense of duty and I lay there in the sterile whiteness of a ward surrounded by strangers.

I was taken almost immediately to the labour ward, after the usual form filling and endless questions. As far as I could make out, this long room was divided by flimsy screens into a series of cubicles. I was in the end cubicle. On the wall hung a blackboard and as each step in labour took place, a nurse filled in the exact time with a piece of squeaky chalk. Every now and again a figure in crackling starched white floated across the open end of my little compartment. I was frightened, and my fright was intensified by the fact that I could not ask what was going on. I doubt if they would have told me even if I had.

I was very thirsty, but when at last an English-speaking nurse looked in on me and I begged for some water, I was told I couldn't drink. It would be bad for me.

Now and again I heard softer movements and the bustle around some other mother; there were moans and less often a scream.

Every hour a doctor and six students came in to examine me. I was still in labour and it finally became apparent that something was very wrong. After twenty-seven hours, the serious discussion between the doctor and the students was resolved into decision. There were a few sharp orders given and the English-speaking nurse pushed past these attendants to stand by me. She translated, 'The doctor says you must try hard to have this baby ... it has gone too long ... you have cramp of the womb.'

The scare those words gave me was sufficient to break the tension cramps as no inducing drugs could have done. The hours of lonely misery were suddenly over and I wasn't alone

71

any longer. Now there was a tiny 'someone' quite close to me. That wee scrap of infant son was to be my reason for hanging onto life in the next years. Were it not for him, and later his brother Christopher Emil, I think I never could have survived the horror which was to follow.

I was confined to the hospital for an unusually long time because the birth had been so difficult. It was fourteen days before I was released. I didn't mind though. There were feeding times to look forward to, when I could hold my little son Michael in my arms and wonder, as most mothers do, at the tiny features and fingers.

Feeding times were heralded by a nurse wheeling a large trolley of the tea cart type. On each shelf of it was placed a row of babies and on the top of the first row was yet another layer of babies at right angles, and over these a white cloth.

In the wards the babies were taken to their respective mothers, and great was my delight and pride when, each time, the nurse asked, 'Whose is this large black one?' – referring to Michael's hair. Michael, because he was the largest, was unfortunately for him always at the bottom of the pile, and the exceptionally long black hair which grew part-way down to his shoulders was certainly something to comment about.

My dearest wish was to show off my new possession to my parents and brother. Everyone else in the ward had relatives to visit them except me. These times were lonely times and, apart from the twenty-five words each month on a very small Red Cross form to my parents, I could neither write to them nor could they write to me. The telegraphic wording was not adequate in any case to describe all I wanted to tell them about my baby, their first grandchild.

We had a different and rather pleasant awakening on the first Sunday in Advent. In most hospitals all over the world patients are brought unwillingly to reality very early in the morning by the clatter of wash bowls and the busy and aseptic routine of the nurses and aides. There are few who have not questioned at some time the system which, while advocating sleep and rest for the sick, awakens its patients at the crack of dawn with a flurry and bustle. The man or woman who has tossed through

72

the dim and frightening night with only the spot-lighted, white-uniformed back of a night nurse and her desk for companionship, and who has just dropped off into an uneasy sleep, must abhor the fresh vigour of youthful nurses bent on rousing patients to a renewed battle with the long and sterile day.

On this particular morning the wards remained in darkness except for the table lamps of the night nurses. It was very quiet ... and then in the distance we heard the sound of singing. Nearer and nearer it came and then, through the open door, we saw the shadows of the singers cast on the corridor wall Seconds later a long procession of nurses, each one carrying a candle, passed slowly by. The beautiful melody and words which they sang '*Schlafe, mein Prinzlein, schlaf ein*' (sleep, my little one, sleep) will always be connected in my mind with the birth of my eldest son.

Not so pleasant is the memory of loud voices coming from the small room adjoining our ward. While the six women, including myself, in my ward were wondering what was going on, a very red-faced nurse emerged from the room, looking intensely indignant. One of us asked her what was the matter. Bitterly and with flaming cheeks, she told us that a twelve-year-old girl had just given birth to an illegitimate baby and in a high-handed tone demanded some service or other. On being told that it was not available, she had precociously startled the nurse by saying, 'I am a German mother, if you don't attend to it immediately I will report you.'

All the mothers in the ward were in entire sympathy with the nurse, although none of us dared say anything openly. The expression on our faces, however, indicated that we all felt the application of a hand on the girl's small rear would not have been amiss in the circumstances.

One of the women in our ward was a born comic and kept us amused. She never seemed to be downhearted, even though she had a kidney ailment. As a consequence she was put on a strict vegetable diet, which she hated. She was enormously fat and, oddly enough, she had the smallest baby among us. When the nurse was present she always looked very demure, as if butter wouldn't melt in her mouth; but the instant the nurse headed for the door, her eyes began to gleam with mischief as she scrambled out of bed and, from her locker, revealed a little round white beanie hat, which she placed on her head. Next, she produced from some hidden source in her locker a tidbit of some sort, either cake or a bun, and between mouthfuls she would treat us to a little dance round the ward.

She was notoriously funny, for the hospital gowns were the usual 'shorties' tied up at the back and the sight of this enormous mountain of flesh with her tremendous thighs protruding from under the gown, plus the ridiculous hat, sent us into transports of laughter.

But, fat as she was, she could move pretty fast when those nearest the door warned the approach of a member of the staff. Off came the hat and into bed she whisked, apparently none the worse for her outing, although I have no doubt the doctors were somewhat at a loss to account for the effects of the unauthorised goodies she ate, which must have played havoc with her diet.

I remember I wanted so badly to be discharged from the hospital because I wanted my little son to myself, away from the strict regime; but I must have been weaker than I thought because even with the shortage of beds I was kept there longer than normal.

Finally, on rather wobbly legs, I traversed the corridor to the discharge office and grabbed the baby's clothes and blankets I had brought with me. I passed my papers into the hatch, and after a few minutes the hatch re-opened and I held my arms out for my baby. Michael was all mine now.

Home in our large room in Frau Lässig's apartment, it didn't take long for me to realise how lucky I was. Despite being rough and ready, rarely smiling, never hearing a gentle word from her, she had a heart of gold. My evenings were never lonely, for when I tired of reading she let me sit with her family and listen to the radio or talk with them. If for any reason I didn't go into her living room after Michael was asleep, she would knock on the door and demand to know why. It was as though I had become part of the family.

Of course Michael was a comfort; what baby isn't? To me he was something special.

The news I heard on the radio shocked me because I could only hear the German stations, which magnified the victories of the Germans, leaving me to imagine the worst. The day it was reported that the 'great harbour of Margate' had been defeated, I realised that all we were hearing was not fact.

The Lässig family had a small garden about a mile from the apartment, which was kept in trim by this indomitable woman, who dug, hoed, and grew vegetables and fruit for her family, even mucking out the pig pen. One pig was raised to slaughter for her family, the other two were for an army officer in a nearby barracks who kept her supplied with plate scrapings, etc.

Thus taking on the extra work was compensated for by all these scraps from the barracks which fed all three pigs so that they cost her nothing for upkeep. Each morning, rain, sunshine or snow, she scurried off (she never walked, always ran) with her full bucket of scraps. On washdays she took a little hand-cart, the kind which practically every German household possesses, loaded not only with the bucket but with a huge wet wash as well. She hung this in the garden to dry, fed her pigs and her Belgian hares, did some gardening and tidying up; and, in about two hours, trotted back to the apartment loaded with sweet-smelling, folded linens.

On her return, she usually prepared for herself a plate of beer soup (which I never tackled) unless I had already cooked something else for her. We both cooked on the same stove and, contrary to the theory that two women should never use the same kitchen, we never quarrelled.

Her method of cooking was somewhat unique. She gave it the least of her attention and it was no unusual thing for her to burn the contents of the pot. One morning I was highly interested when I saw her take a pot of rice from the stove when it had only just come to the boil. She immediately wrapped the pot in a thick wad of newspaper, tied it in a blanket and then told Lotte to 'put it to bed'. This was new to me but it proved also to be her most successful method of cooking rice, beans, peas or lentils.

By the time they sat down to dinner everything was of just the right tenderness after a day 'in bed'. The bed coverings here, as in most of Germany, consisted of a huge puffy feather-filled envelope which covered the entire bed. This method of cooking worked on the same basis as the old haybox. Quite often, before she trotted off in the mornings, I would ask her what she wanted me to cook for her, but she usually shrugged off this question with the remark, 'Stand a pot of water on the stove about two hours before dinner, we will find something to put into it.' Thus, Mrs Beeton's recipes commencing with 'take twenty eggs' were out and Frau Lässig's recipes 'take a pot of water' were in.

In German households in those days it was rare for the women to do washing each week. Each block of apartments was equipped with a wash 'kitchen' in the basement. This room was stone or cement floored with a drain in the middle and a large stone boiler in the corner It was usually rather dark. One of the tenants was put in charge of this facility and it was her duty to see that the tenants had the use of it on an amicable rota. She also saw to it that the persons using it were out at the proper time and that everything was left spotless and dry.

The outcome of the rota meant that each family did its washing about every eight weeks and that the washroom was allotted to each apartment for three days at a time. After eight weeks the mound of laundry reached formidable heights and when it came to my turn, even though there was only washing for myself and the baby, I was awed by it.

The first day as I struggled to heave the heavy, wet enormous covers used to envelop the feathered quilt, Frau Lässig scuttled in and, pushing me away, said roughly, 'Oh go away, let me do it properly.'

From that day on I always had her to help me. Refusing any form of recompense, she would rush in and tackle my problems. She also allowed me to take my clean wet laundry on her handcart out to the garden, which I usually managed by pushing the baby buggy in front of me and pulling the cart behind.

Among other economies brought about by lack of gasoline for civilian purposes was that the coal briquets used for heating the big tile ovens were not delivered to individual homes during the war. The consignment of coal was brought to the coal yards in trucks and the coal was unloaded into huge heaps. The women then took their handcarts to the yards, and on presentation of ration cards the amount of coal per person in the family was weighed and thrown into a separate heap. It was then a daylong task and a heavy dirty one to load up the carts and drag them back and forth to the apartments until the heaps were gone.

The tenant of each apartment had a small partitioned-off space in the basement to be used for storing wood, coal and potatoes. The coal briquets had to be stacked neatly from floor to ceiling to ensure there was room left for anything else; the 'anything else' included the tenants when they were forced to take refuge in the confined spaces left when the air-raid alarm was sounded.

Frau Lässig would never allow me to do this piling job and also insisted on pulling the cart back and forth for me. As well as myself, there was another tenant in the Lässig apartment occupying a second single room. This man, Herr Baier, had his meals supplied by Frau Lässig. I never learned much about him except that he was a hairdresser and that he had his permanent home in the Saalfeld region. Nor did I know the reason for his not being conscripted. He was quite friendly and sat with us in the evenings, but he rarely spoke about his activities and I supposed he had a health problem exempting him from conscription.

This was the household into which I had moved days before my baby was born. The week before I moved I was still without furniture or bedding. Luck was with me, however, in that after searching in practically every district in Leipzig without success for a bed, I found a little store in a back street and the owner told me he had some furniture which had been ordered by a man who had been conscripted and had cancelled his order because his wife had returned to her parents' home. The owner now had the furniture on his hands. I was only too delighted with this stroke of luck and became the proud possessor of a large double bed, two bedside tables, a dresser and wardrobe, a kitchen table with pull-out space for washing-up bowls, two kitchen and two bedroom chairs, and a large kitchen cabinet. Even with this amount of furniture in the very large room there was still ample space.

All I needed now was the bedding, and this proved more difficult. The normal clothing cards included no bedding, which had to be obtained from the rationing office in the form of special vouchers. Facing the officials in such an office was never pleasant. The men especially chosen for this sort of work didn't give an inch they didn't have to. I explained the position. I explained that I was expecting a baby and that I was moving into an unfurnished apartment. The answer I got was not helpful.

'When you have moved in we can consider it.'

'But,' I argued, 'if I move in I can't sleep without bed-clothes.'

'That is your problem, madam,' was the unfeeling answer. I became very angry. It got me nowhere. Finally I tried being pathetic.

'Do you want me, an expectant mother, to sleep on bare boards?' I pleaded.

I had hit on the right note. The man with whom I was speaking went over to another officer and, after a long discussion with this official during which from time to time they both came to the door of the office to look me over, I was given a voucher entitling me to sheeting – I had to make this up myself into pillow slips and duvet covers – and an extra voucher for feathers.

The big sheeting slips were like enormous pillow cases and would be unwieldy to sew, but at that stage I was so glad to have won my battle with red tape that I was triumphant. But still I wasn't finished with my requirements.

'The baby?' I asked.

'What about the baby?'

'I am going into hospital next week and shall need bedding for the baby.'

'First the baby, then the bedding, madam,' the official said firmly, a steely glint in his eye.

I tried pleading. No good. I pleaded to him as a husband and a father, if indeed he was a husband and father. No good.

Finally I said firmly, 'Then I shall stay here until I do get it. And curtains for the room as well,' I added as an afterthought. If I was going to have a fight, then I considered it might as well cover everything at once instead of in instalments.

'Oh no! *No, no, no, gnädige Frau!* Definitely NO!' said the man, and left me standing. I walked over and sat on a bench. Every now and again he glanced out of the corner of his eye to see if I were still there. I was. I saw that no one was going to break, so I tried other methods. Quietly I started to sob. On and on I wept; softly, but heartbreakingly. After a time I noticed that he was moving towards the door of the inner office and finally he emerged with his superior and beckoned to me.

'We have decided to make an exception,' he announced, thrillingly. I thanked him. He wrote out vouchers covering a baby's needs – *and* the curtains ... I took the papers from him and walked wearily to the door. Once out of sight, however, I ran. I ran in spite of my condition, as fast as I could in the direction of the huge department store known as 'Knoops'. Earlier I had seen a consignment of curtain goods and I wanted to make sure I got there before the store closed. If I didn't I was only too well aware I might have to wait months for the next consignment. There was no choice of anything in the store but the novel experience of buying such a large quantity of anything was really enjoyable. Luckily there was a bus stop close by my home, for the parcels were heavy and bulky.

The next day, while speaking to Frau Lässig again, she told me to have the furniture delivered immediately and to bring the parcels of bedding to her and she would make it all up for me. I said I could do it if she would lend me her sewing machine.

'You can't do all that heavy sewing with a treadle machine in your condition,' she said, and that was her final word.

Before the end of the month she had finished everything.

There are special stores to be found in every German town equipped with huge machines with dials on them. I chose the type of feathers I wanted, the softest down for the baby's and regular feathers for mine. The openings in the envelopes were pulled over a funnel and presto! the required weight of the feathers was puffed into the envelopes, which were quickly stitched up by the girl in charge. While waiting for this to be done I noticed that there was a machine which sucked out feathers, cleaned them and puffed them back. All very different to what I had been used to in England.

So it was that Michael and I settled into our new home. We did everything together. We even visited an art exhibition together and Michael 'chose' a picture for me for Mother's Day. At least I pretended he chose it for me. What actually happened, of course, was that the subject of the picture was a large white horse and Michael just loved horses. He does to this day. I still have the picture hanging in our home. It has travelled a long way since then but I wouldn't part with it again. When we left Leipzig later, I left it with a cousin. When the Russians occupied Leipzig she sold it with the other furniture. Later, following an enquiry from me, she bought the picture back and sent it to my present parents-in-law in Gera. When they escaped from their home in the East Zone some years later, this picture was put at the bottom of the only piece of luggage they took with them and brought to the West Zone. When Michael visited them in the summer of 1957, just before we emigrated to Canada, he returned home with the picture in his rucksack.

9

When Michael was three weeks old, my mother-in-law invited me to go to Steisslingen for Christmas. Both she and her parents were anxious to see the baby and, although transportation and distance forecast a nightmarish journey, I accepted.

Apart from the discomfort of travel in wartime, the darkened railway stations were depressing, eerie, and gave a sense of unreality to everything. The gay atmosphere of pre-war years, when holiday-bound travellers laughed and chatted in pleasant anticipation, was gone, and the once eager blasts of engine whistles now shrilled an eldritch warning note. Even nostalgic good-byes at open carriage doors were a thing of the past. When the surging mass of humanity had battled its way onto the train, every inch of space was fought for. Those who had by dint of sharp elbows obtained the enviable comfort of a place on the hard wooden seats provided on the continental trains were little better off than those who stood in the packed corridors as they were squeezed tightly together. On this battlefield there was certainly no time, or room, for extended farewells or for waving handkerchiefs.

With a baby in my arms and a case in my hand, this scrambling departure from Leipzig main station was even more arduous. Again, we had to change at Weissenfels, not too far distant from Leipzig, and I remembered the last time I had made this trip and how cold that station had been; then I wondered how I would manage with the case and the large bundle of baby in my arms. An additional worry was I had not healed from being stitched after the birth.

Michael, on the other hand, seemed quite happy with his lot. He was warmly clad and, in addition, I was carrying him, in the practical way the Germans have, in his own pillow.

Pillows on the Continent are large and square, not the oblong shape which is standard in English-speaking countries. The method of carrying a baby is to stand the pillow on one of its edges and to push down the opposite top edge, forming a boat-shaped depression. The baby is placed in this hollow and is then immune from cold as it is almost completely enveloped in feathery softness; no little foot sticking out and no chance of a shawl sliding down to let in a draught.

At Weissenfels I was lucky, I found a small space in the waiting room. When the train did steam in I wondered how I would manage, for I certainly could not negotiate the steep steps up into the coach, hampered as I was. I need not have worried. As I stood looking up at the crowded door, several soldiers stretched out helpful hands and hauled us both up and I pushed my way through to a coach marked 'MOTHER & CHILD'.

It was crowded and I stood outside until a woman in a uniform came along. She took one quick authoritative look into the coach, tapped a woman on her shoulder and said curtly, 'Out'. It was quite apparent that the woman was not legitimately on the coach from the way she muttered 'excuse me' as she hurried past me. I sat in her place.

The coach was in total darkness and when Michael's wailing informed me that nappy changing could not be put off any longer, I found that the operation required a combination of sleight of hand and blind man's buff. The wonder is that I got the nappy on Michael and not on one of the other tightly squeezed in passengers in the compartment. It was touch and go. There was no elbow room, for the compartment was stuffed to capacity with women and children. Children were even sleeping on the floor and the smaller ones slept in the luggage nets above our heads.

It was a relief to arrive in Stuttgart, and this time we awaited our connection in the 'MOTHER & CHILD' waiting room. Here everything was provided necessary for the comfort of children. Nurses were in attendance; food, milk, cots and baths were supplied. Nothing was forgotten.

My mother-in-law met us at Singen station and, of course,

made much of her grandson. When we arrived at the house his great-grandparents could not take their eyes from him. All in all, it was a pleasant time that Christmas. It was peaceful and the village went about its way as though there were not a war in progress.

In January I left with Michael for Leipzig, where we remained until the summer. Michael was a reasonably good baby, but it was always a source of amusement to the Lässig family and myself when the radio was turned on for one of Hitler's speeches (which unfortunately was very often). Michael immediately gurgled, gave a wriggle and promptly fell off to sleep. I doubt if many babies have ever been soothed to sleep with such a raucous lullaby.

I had not worked at the Berlitz School since just before the baby was born, but the lack of income was no hardship. Mothers and babies were well taken care of in Germany. We received from the Government not only the rent in those days, but payment of light and heating. In addition, all bills for the baby's needs, such as for the cot, bedding, bath, pram, etc. had to be submitted to the Government, who paid them all.

The allowance received by a wife whose husband was at the front could be used entirely for food and clothing, which, of course, were regulated by the point system. As far as housework was concerned, there was very little to do once I had cleaned and tidied our room. This left me with plenty of time to take Michael for long walks, with a visit every two weeks to the Zoo, for which Leipzig was famous, having at that time, it was said, the largest collection of lions in the world.

News of consignments of vegetables, which were unrationed, spread quickly. This meant that one had to drop whatever one was doing, rush to the greengrocer's and wait, sometimes for as long as two hours, in order to receive perhaps two oranges, although such fruit was rarely obtainable, and for children only.

During my Christmas visit to Steisslingen, great-grandmother Xaveria had introduced Michael to a comforter, one of those rubber teat things used in days gone by to keep babies quiet. It was no good my arguing, she was persistent and

Michael was only too delighted to go along with this treat.

In this case Michael's comforter was even more unsanitary than most, for often when I came into the room I'd catch great-grandmother retrieving it from the floor beneath a cupboard. She'd then dust it off on her skirt and pop it back into his mouth again. Complaining did no good, she merely brushed me off as if I didn't know what I was talking about. Finally she hit on a really 'splendid' idea as far as she and the baby were concerned, one she thought the height of luxury. She started dipping the comforter into honey. Of course Michael really appreciated this treat and sucked away happily. It was not until I was en route for Leipzig that I awoke to the fact that honey was only available in the country and either his breaking of the habit was going to be rudely abrupt, or I would have to find a substitute.

Consultation with Frau Lässig resulted in a temporary solution. She suggested that I ask at the drug store for a concoction known as Eibischsaft. This worked very well for a while until I went to buy my third bottle of the liquid. The druggist, a man with no sense of humour whatsoever, looked at me over his spectacles and said, 'Madam, if your child still has his cough I suggest that you try something a little more. potent.' The syrup he handed me this time was horrible, as was indicated by Michael's small screwed-up face as he spat it out, and for a few days we suffered the miseries of a small boy screaming his head off for that which it was impossible to produce.

The next summer I travelled south again and this time my mother-in-law showed herself for what she really was, a hard, calculating woman. My baby was turned over to his great-grandmother entirely, and I was turned over to working in the many fields owned by his great-grandfather. Here, in the south, farmhouses were not built with their fields compactly around them, as they are in English-speaking countries. The farmhouses were in the village itself and a farmer might own fields as many as eight miles away, scattered in all directions. Thus, before working a field for any purpose, there was quite a distance to go and one usually travelled on a bicycle. And those roads were rutted and rough. The fields on each side were never enclosed by a hedge or fence, they were open on all sides.

It was hard work, and the sun beat down unmercifully. We had to drag six-foot wooden rakes over the rough stubble in the heat of day. There was no shade, very little rest, and in the evenings as our reward, sour bread, raw onion and hard cider. Yet there were other foods to be had by illicit exchange.

We traded our tobacco rations for eggs or meat, the schnapps which we brewed ourselves we exchanged for clothing and butter. But, apart from the baby, who had good milk and butter, we got none of the good things, for my mother-in-law preserved everything else which came into her hands, even part of her own rations ... 'All for Carlie'. Even the strawberries in the garden were bottled for him. I often saw great-grandfather sneaking into his own garden in the half-light of the morning to steal a few raspberries or strawberries for himself. He must have been afraid of his daughter's tongue, or maybe it was that at his age (he was well over eighty) he wanted to avoid any arguments.

One of the main items we used for exchange purposes, for any food or clothing we needed, was liqueurs. We made these ourselves from schnapps, which we also distilled. In the deep cool cellar of the farmhouse there was an enormous barrel in the corner. Into this went any fruit – apples, pears, plums – not good enough for eating. The barrel was covered with several thick horse-blankets. Adding fruit to the mess already in the barrel was not undertaken lightly. Each horse-blanket was lifted at one corner until only one remained. Then that one was swiftly lifted and the fruit popped in simultaneously. Even then the heady fermenting gases were strong enough to cause one to back off in a hurry.

Once a year when the revenue man came to the village, the barrel, by now filled with fermenting fruit, was eased up the stairs and onto a cart pulled by oxen and then taken to a still in the forest. The revenue officer was in constant attendance while it operated, but it was fairly easy for my mother-in-law to hold him in conversation while I tapped a few illegal jugs of the crystal fluid. This extra schnapps helped us to get many items we would have otherwise had to do without.

Perhaps it was that the official turned a blind eye to what was going on, for we weren't the only ones getting away with it by any means. Most of the residents of the village had their private store. This extra schnapps was just right for making liqueur and the process was relatively simple. We gathered wild strawberries or raspberries, placed them in clear glass jars, poured schnapps onto them and then the jars were covered. These we stood on a windowsill in the sun for about two months.

Quite often we noticed that the normal level was no longer even and that the mixture lipped up the side of the glass; then great-grandfather had to watch out or he would get the sharp edge of his daughter's tongue. I noticed him many times creeping past, picking up a jar, having a sip and then hurriedly replacing the lid, hoping that his sampling would go unnoticed.

When the day's work was done in the fields there was still the housework, and this was no easy chore. The inside stable doors opened into the front passage of the house and great-grandfather's dragging steps usually brought with them a goodly coating of straw and manure. He also had a habit of sitting at the kitchen table and coaxing the hens with some tidbit or other into the kitchen through the open back door. Consequently scrubbing was a daily job. Washing up pots was also difficult. All water had to be heated up on the huge iron stove fuelled by wood faggots. Then the rims of the saucepans (each pan had a wide rim all round the outside about three inches from the bottom that was set over the holes in the top of the stove) became coated with soot from contact with the flames. These saucepans were heavy and cumbersome and had to be held away from the person carrying them, to avoid the sooty bases from coming into contact with any clothing. Soap-filled pads, or even steel wool, were an unheard-of commodity. We had to take a twist of straw and scrub. Elbow grease and patience were the two items most necessary for a gleaming pot in that kitchen. Neither my hands nor the hands of any of the women in the neighbourhood could have been used for one of the ever-popular 'mother/daughter' commercials we see so much of today; soft hands were unknown.

On Saturdays the whole house was cleaned from top to bottom, windows, walls and floors. It was scrub, rub and polish from morning to night, and after supper every house in the village sent one of its occupants out onto the road with a broom to sweep. Each farmer, with no exception, kept his side of the road clean as far as the imaginary centre line, so that on Sunday morning the roads bore a reasonably sanitary aspect.

These houses had no bathtubs, although a few boasted an old-fashioned hip-bath. Generally though, baths were considered to be unhealthy and at least the older inhabitants believed that only imbeciles bent on catching cold took them.

There was, however, apart from the bathroom in the doctor's house and in the *Schloss* (occupied by a titled family, with whom I never came in contact), one bath in the village with proper plumbing and that was above the baker's premises. Here, for the sum of fifty pfennig, I could take Michael and indulge in a glorious soak. I never had any bother hiring it; for that matter, I never saw anyone else or heard of anyone else taking advantage of, to me, this de luxe convenience.

It was not long before I discovered that my mother-in-law did not have a very good reputation in the village. She was well-known for her boasting, bragging and lying and also for her not too moral ways. Her marriage to Carl's father had ended in divorce several years before. The reason, according to her, was that he had drunk to excess; but while riffling through a photograph album one day, I found a photo of her present husband dated well before the divorce. Certainly she had kept Carl when they separated, but of course it would have been because his father had no means of keeping a child and there were, in those days, no such things as court custody orders.

When she married Repp, her present husband, he hadn't adopted Carl, so my husband's name was still Baun. I was so unhappy living with his mother and having to cope with her domineering ways that one day, in sheer desperation, I ventured up to the house of the parish priest. Almost every family in the village was Roman Catholic and, as I was Church of England, I was not quite sure whether I was doing the right thing or not in visiting Father Stroebel. But I was desperate for someone to whom I could talk.

We chatted for a while and then he said suddenly, 'Your child, of course, was baptised in the Catholic Church?'

'No, he wasn't.'

'But his father is Catholic.'

'Yes, I know, but his mother isn't.'

'Well! We won't quarrel about it.'

He smiled, and from that moment on we became firm friends. I could always go to him when things became too much for me.

At about that same time I made more friends. A man by the name of Dr Paul Wohlheim asked me if I would give English lessons to his daughter Doris, when I could get away from the fields. His wife, who was a doctor in her own right, welcomed me into her home and it was heaven to get away onto the hill on which their pretty house stood. The house with its chintz curtains, polished wood, beautiful furniture and library of books, was so different from the farmhouse. After giving Doris her lesson in the nursery, I could come down and sit on the terrace in the quiet of the evening with her mother and look at the peaceful countryside; it was as refreshing as a cool glass of water.

My mother-in-law was angry because I was invited there and she wasn't. There was usually trouble before I went and still more when I returned, but it was worth it. Because she wished to make a good impression on the doctor's family (she felt herself socially above the normal run of farmers), she never refused them when they asked me to go there; but afterwards she complained bitterly because she was never invited.

Sometimes, on particularly dark evenings when we were sitting in the farm kitchen, we would hear a soft tapping on the back door. The very fact that the knocking came at the back and not on the front door was sufficient for us to put out the light immediately, for we knew it would be one or two of the French prisoners-of-war confined in the village.

When they had first been brought to the village, they were always confined in a house opposite the village hall; but later it was found that they could be useful on the farms in the absence of some of the farmers and their sons. They were thus given comparative freedom during the daytime and were only locked in at night. However, as with most prisoners-of-war, if they had the least opportunity of getting out after lock-up they took it.

At these times they visited houses where they knew they would not be given away and where, more often than not, they knew the occupants listened to news from other countries. It was their only way of knowing what was going on in the world outside. Several of them also made plans of escape while in our house for, after all, they were only a few miles from the Swiss frontier. They improvised home-made compasses, they drew up maps; and much discussion was given as to the best method of evading the frontier guards.

While I was there on this visit, seven of them made the attempt. Two got away and five were recaptured and never heard from again. One day a farmer brought the news that the bee-keeper's hut had been broken into and white coats taken. It was some years after the war when I was reading *The Colditz Story* that I discovered that two English prisoners-of-war had been the culprits, using the white coats to get them over the border in a snowy landscape. Shortly after that episode, all French prisoners-of-war were transferred from the area.

Now and again on a Sunday, I took Michael down to the lake and 'swam' him about on my hands. He was very hardy and loved it, although the water was very cold. He was only a few months old and after his dip lay on the grass while I swam far out to the middle of the lake. I liked to dream in those moments, pretending that we were on holiday and that there was no work to be done, no war, no farm, no mother-in-law, just Michael, the water, the forest, the wayside cross above the orchard on the road, and me. I am afraid on these occasions, the peasants, as they took their Sunday walks in their long drab clothing, looked askance at us. A woman in her bathing costume and swimming! They considered this dangerous and unhealthy and I was, I am sure in their minds, contravening all decency.

10

Then one day we received a message from Carl. He had telephoned the village store, owned by the *Bürgermeister*, that he
would be arriving at a village some distance from Steisslingen
and asked if I would meet him there. The only way to fetch
him was on a bicycle, using one hand for steering and the other
to tow a second bicycle. This was hardly a problem, except
for balance, as there were no main roads to negotiate. My
mother-in-law made no bones about it that, in her estimation,
mothers were far more important to their sons than their wives.
I was to remain and complete a good job of cleaning in order
for all to be spick and span for his arrival.

I wasn't particularly averse to the arrangements, for by this
time I had realised that Carl and I were entirely unsuited to
one another. His propensity for lying was still apparent in his
letters, none of which rang true. When he did arrive in the
house he seemed pleased enough to see me, but it was made
quite obvious by his mother that I was an intruder. Finally,
during the evening, she started making sneering references to
my parents (who of course she did not know), to the fact that
I was homesick (a fact which I had never admitted to myself,
let alone allowed it to be seen by others), and then she
launched into the subject of the village girls, of his past conquests, and of the possible future conquests he might make
during his present leave. I could bear no more and left the
room and the house.

Somehow I had to get away from this 'sticky' atmosphere.
I wandered down to the lakeshore, tossing and turning in my
mind what I could do. Carl followed me, but made no excuses
for the upset. I, however, told him that things could not go on
as they were and that for both our sakes it would be better to

part right away. This seemed not to disturb him unduly and it was probably obvious that he had already discussed the matter with his mother. He calmly remarked that, according to German law, if I refused to give him another child he could divorce me and could take Michael away from me. That was the deciding point.

I agreed to carry on. I hoped that matters would improve, but I begged him to consider leaving with me for Leipzig for the last half of his leave, where we could be alone in order that we might have a chance to try and understand one another better. I could not risk losing my baby.

Surprisingly enough he agreed and, a week before he was due to leave for the front, we left Singen en route for Leipzig. It was a relief to be away from the farm, but the time was short and there is little I can remember of those few days except the day he left. In the afternoon he went out alone and returned with a present for me. My heart turned over when I saw that it was a jet necklace. I am not superstitious, and yet the sight of the black shiny beads struck me as an omen. He told me that he had been unable to get anything else, that was all he could find.

We carried Michael to the *Hauptbahnhof* with us that evening. It was as gloomy as ever, but there was a queer feeling of finality about his going. His last words were, 'If I don't come back for a long time, will you wait? I may try to get over the Russian lines to get out of it all.' I laid no importance to the statement because as usual I felt it to be extravagant. The last I ever saw of him was in the semi-darkness of the platform as the soles of his army boots disappeared through the train window which, with the crush milling around, was the only way into the train carrying the men back to the Russian front.

It didn't take long to realise that another baby was on its way; it was a difficult time – the air raids were such that there was seldom one night in which I didn't have to grab Michael and rush to the cellar. There we sat on the heaps of potatoes stored there and waited for the planes to go over, with the subsequent relief of the 'all clear' signal.

Preparing for these nightly visitations from the skies became quite an art. First I folded our clothes and placed them in a neat pile on the top of my shoes. Michael's buggy I stood near the door with the cover turned back and a thermos of his formula ready packed in the bottom of it. I put in an extra rug over the handles of the buggy and big muslin nappies already dipped in water and wrung out so that they were damp; this was in the case of fire, to protect the baby from the worst of it. It became a matter of two minutes to be all prepared and at the top of the cellar stairs waiting for someone to help me down with the buggy.

I dressed Michael once we were down there. One evening the alarm went quite early, around seven o'clock. I had just put my week's allowance of meat on the stove (about half a pound of rather tough stewing beef). As usual, the saucepan was first filled three-quarters with water and I was sitting in the Lässig's room listening to the radio. Frau Lässig was out, but her husband and daughter were there. When the alarm went, we followed the usual procedure for safety and Herr Lässig took up his post with the other fire-watchers upstairs in the attic.

About two and a half hours later the 'all clear' sounded but we were told to stay where we were. The fire-watchers smelled something burning and were searching for the source, thinking it may be a *Brandbombe* or fire bomb. They found it quite soon when they opened the Lässig apartment door; clouds of black smoke met them. It was, however, no *Brandbombe*, but my week's dinner – a burned offering; black as charcoal and the saucepan burned beyond repair. This was just another of the minor casualties of war.

In March, my mother-in-law came to visit me, although I didn't delude myself that it was me she wanted to see. I was determined that somehow or other I would manage to be pleasant to her. Bickering wasn't worth while and, after all, one couldn't change the situation. But she had barely been in the room a day when she began telling me of all the girls my husband might have or should have married and, in my condition and after so many sleepless nights, it was very stressful. She left immediately and went upstairs to my aunt's apartment, where I feel sure she got a sympathetic hearing.

The next day she left for Steisslingen. Looking back, it may be that the nervous tensions, fears and pressures of the times magnified ills, wrongs and slights in both our minds. Perhaps under more normal circumstances we could have been friends, but somehow I doubt it.

The circumstances in which I was living made me not quite so accepting as I had been. Frau Lässig had, during this time, grown so fond of Michael and me that I always had someone to talk to, to be kind to me, and to give me advice.

Now, each morning I took Michael for an airing in his stroller and accompanied Frau Lässig to her garden. We both watched with interest when the Belgian hares she kept had their litters and we were very amused at one of them. This particular hare had two litters and on each occasion had made a beautiful nest prior to the birth, but once the babies were born she left them in the middle of the cage and wouldn't feed them. Frau Lässig, with a grim look on her face wagged a warning finger at 'bunny' and remarked, 'All right, my girl, once more and if you don't look after them this time, in the pot you go.'

A few weeks later we found another beautiful nest awaiting the arrival of a litter and, sure enough, the day after, when we looked into the cage there were the babies, stranded as usual, weakly struggling in their blindness, while their mother turned a scornful back on them. To my amazement, Frau Lässig opened the door of the cage, grabbed the big hare by the ears and smacked her firmly twice across the mouth. The hare shook her head and then hopped across, picked up each baby, placed it in the nest until they were all settled, and then she started placidly to feed them. Apparently the lesson had done the trick.

On July 1, 1943 there was a tap on my door early in the morning. Frau Lässig came in, and in her rough but kindly voice said, 'I'm taking my grandchildren to the Zoo today, now don't you go having that baby until I get back.'

I thought this rather a comical remark as I couldn't have

much to say about it. I had, however, made arrangements with a midwife, a woman who lived in the same block of apartments, to come in and attend to me. I had refused to go to hospital for I was afraid of leaving Michael alone. This meant that I would have to dispense with a doctor too, for doctors outside the hospital were becoming a rarity; those left were usually fully occupied coping with the casualties in the bombed areas.

I was quite satisfied with my arrangement to have this woman attend to me with Frau Lässig's help, and the thought of being alone for the day didn't worry me. I settled down to amusing Michael. He was just at the cute stage, cuddly and affectionate, and he prattled away incessantly to me. By four o'clock, however, I was sure that the baby was on its way and was very glad when at five o'clock Frau Lässig bustled in with a, 'Well, I hope you have behaved yourself, my girl.'

She took one look at me and then began to make preparations. Michael was put to bed in her room, she called the midwife, and the two of them sat down at my kitchen table to wait out the events.

During the war, when real coffee was a rarity, each midwife was allowed a special ration of it to help her through the night watches. The delightful aroma of the brew that the two women were sharing swirled around me as they talked. Occasionally they included me in their conversation and now and again checked my comfort.

Naturally, following the visit to the Zoo, the talk revolved around what my landlady had seen and heard and it is still vivid in my memory, the horror I felt when she said she had heard that a small child had fallen into the hippo enclosure the day before and been killed. Whether it was true or not, and whether a hippo will kill a child or not, I never knew and probably shall never find out. I only know that it was possibly the queerest conversation any mother has had to listen to while awaiting the birth of a child.

At four in the morning of July 2, Christopher was born, and when two hours later Michael was brought in to be given the new 'present', he was delighted. The baby became his dearest possession; he would go nowhere without him. And woe betide any fatuous neighbour who dared say, 'I think I'd like to have that little brother of yours.' This called forth all the fury that a small eighteen-month-old can muster.

We announced the birth over the radio in the hope that someone would pass it on to my husband at the front, and a telegram was sent to his field unit. Another telegram was sent off to Paul Broglie in Switzerland, for I knew he would, in turn, advise my parents as soon as he could. Carl must have received the news, for about a week later I had a letter from him acknowledging it. It was the last letter I ever received from him.

Months later, it was reported that Carl was officially missing as of July 11, 1943, nine days after Christopher was born. Letters took a long time from the front. Weeks went by with no news, and then one day a card arrived advising me that a parcel awaited me at the post office.

Frau Lässig looked at me rather queerly, but she said nothing. At the post office I was handed the parcel and, as I took it, Carl's pipe fell from a split in the paper. I took it, sat down on a bench and turned it over and over. Because of the shock, it was quite a long time before I saw stamped on the wrappings: *'Property of a wounded soldier'*.

When I got home I opened it. There was very little inside except his diary and a few letters – some from me and some from his mother – and some handkerchiefs. In order to find out approximately where he had been, I read through some of the letters and, to my horror, discovered one from his mother telling him that when he came home on leave he should pick up Michael from Leipzig and take him to visit her. There was no mention of him taking me. She suggested that he could have a grand time with a certain Helga with whom he had once been friends. This was the last straw. The involving of my little son in this sordid mess settled the matter for me. I determined that at the first opportunity I would get my boys and myself back to England.

I was well aware that doing this might take months, even years. Later I received another letter from Carl's company advising he had been wounded in his left arm by a grenade splinter and had been sent back from the front lines to a lazarette. He had, however, never arrived there, and since then they had no news of him. Nor has there ever been, in spite of intensive investigation and searches through Red Cross records.

His company had been situated on the River Oka near Orel in Russia, so much was established from his mail; but by the time it was discovered that he was missing, the German Army was in retreat and nothing could be traced.

That fall and winter were hard. Rationing kept pretty steady but there were many delays with deliveries to wholesalers and retailers when a transport had been bombed. And as an extra obstruction, there were full-blown black market dealings going on.

Queuing became a regular thing, and sometimes what may have seemed humorous were actually battles of wits to obtain every possible article as it became available. On one occasion as I waited in the local grocery store, I saw the assistant slip a tube of toothpaste into the basket of the woman in front of me. Toothpaste was an almost unheard of commodity at that time, but then so were many other things. When it came to my turn, I asked if I might have a tube too. Sourly the assistant looked me over and replied, 'You can either have toothpaste or black shoe polish, but you can't have both.' I supposed I couldn't be clean at both ends, so I chose the former.

Only the older men and very young boys were left at home now. Since many preparations for emergency were ordered to be made, it was therefore the women who had to do the work. Doorways were built adjoining all the cellars of the apartments in the block. The intention of this measure was that if one building was struck, then those in its cellar could break through easily from building to building and effect an escape.

Another government order was that the attics of every building had to be cleared of all surplus material and wood to give fire fighters every opportunity to cope with possible firebombs. Each attic had heavy beams throughout and to these beams laths of wood were nailed. These walls divided the large space into rooms which had been allotted and utilised up to this time by each apartment for storage, and on wet days the washing could be hung up there to dry or air. Now, all the laths and beams had to be removed. We were also reminded that this was wartime and that nails were scarce. As each nail was removed the children had to grade them for size and later the women hammered them straight for further use. After this, they were collected by the town authorities. The laths were reasonably easy to remove, although the prying out of each separate nail made it a painfully long process. The beams were another story, each was about nine inches square and they were from sixteen to eighteen feet long, solid and heavy. There was only one way to bring them down and load them onto trucks for transportation. Three women stood at each of the four landing windows; the beams were then gently eased out of the attic window until they rested on the held-out hands of the women on the floor below. They were then slid down to the next window and so on. For a few weeks after this attic clearance the evenings resounded with hammering from each apartment as nails were straightened.

It was about this time too that Frau Lässig came and warned me to be careful what I said and did. She told me that an official of the Party had come to the door and asked for me. She knew him personally and asked him why. He told her that I had been reported to them for listening to the English stations on the radio. She immediately told him that was impossible. She assured him that hers was the only radio in the apartment and that she was convinced I had never been alone with it. She also added that as a staunch member of the Party she would be only too willing to watch me even more closely and to report me for the slightest slip.

A few weeks later she told me that she had enquired further into the occurrence and found that my own aunt had done some loose and quite unfounded gossiping, leading to the enquiry.

Generally speaking, when planes flew over at night we took it as a foregone conclusion that they would be on their way to

Merseburg to bomb the Leuna chemical works with the great brown-coal mines attached to them, where they made synthetic gasoline. These were only twenty miles from Leipzig, but on the night of December 4, 1943 we were wrong.

Hardly had we sprung from bed at the sound of the first siren than the earth seemed to heave and shake. This time we rushed to the cellar even faster than usual. Some of the children from the upstairs apartments were only half clad and the first thing to do was to get their clothes on. As we worked with shaking fingers to do up reluctant buttons, the crashes and reverberations increased terrifyingly, and when we finally sat ourselves down in our accustomed places, there was a strained look on everyone's face. My main fear was that if we were struck, one of us might be left alone, and so I held Michael on my lap, placing the baby on the top of him, then I bent my body over both of them. In this way I hoped that whatever might happen would happen to all of us together. All that night I repeated over and over, the prayer my mother taught me as a child:

Jesus Tender Shepherd hear us, Bless Thy little lambs tonight; through the darkness be Thou near us; keep us safe till morning light.

The sound of my voice calmed the children. The magnitude of the detonations drove all conversation from our bruised minds, only the blind rote of prayer was possible.

The attacks that night were so bad that the temporary barricades over the openings between the cellars were broken down in readiness. Even down in the cellars we could hear the screaming fear of cattle from Sachs Park, and the crashing and earthquake-like shaking of the walls and floors went on and on; it seemed for an eternity.

Then suddenly, it was quiet. Our watches indicated seven o'clock, but still we sat. No sirens gave the 'all clear'. After a time the men of the fire watch stumbled in, haggard and grey. They said that they thought we could go upstairs now.

One by one we crept to the house door and stood in front

of the main entrance, in disbelief. It was pitch-dark, but there was a red glow in the sky over the centre of the city. The cattle were still bellowing. It should have been growing light, but it wasn't. A deep and murky fog covered everything and it stayed that way for two days. And all the time, softly falling and covering everything with ash were tiny pieces of burned, charred music. Leipzig, once the city of music, was burning. The fire watchers gave their reports. The flares thrown by the planes (Christmas trees as we called them) had lit Leipzig completely, making it an easy target, but those thrown behind the ATG plant, situated across railway tracks about 200 yards from my widow and one of the largest factories in the city, had failed to light, even though this factory had to have been one of their main targets. This had saved our small corner.

Other reports brought in were of terrible devastation in the city itself, but there was nothing we could do that day. By four in the afternoon there was still no daylight. Everyone was numb in mind and body after that terrible bombardment and neither that day nor the next could we gather sufficient initiative to do anything at all. A few of us did drift together in groups to walk into the centre of the city to search for relatives and friends, but it was difficult. There was no organised plan of campaign, we were too drearily apathetic.

I left the babies with a neighbour and walked, or rather scrambled, into the centre of the city with Frau Lässig. High mounds of rubble blocked the streets and the only way from one point to another was to climb over collapsed walls and ruins. Some streets were blocked by fire from wall to wall. It was bitterly cold, and we saw flames licking round huge icicles which hung from shattered buildings. In some cases the glass was boiling, apparently intact in the window frames. Everything was chaos.

Sometimes a twisted tram rail indicated our direction. Streets had disappeared and everywhere sobbing people tried to rescue their loved ones or to search for property among the ruins. Frau Lässig had friends living in a house facing the Thomas Kirche. I remember her remarking as we neared it and saw the church still standing, 'They must be all right or the

100

church would be gone.' But when we reached the spot we found that every house round the church had gone, only the church itself remained. Quietly we turned our backs and as we moved away she muttered, 'Well, that is that!' It wasn't a heartless remark, it was the inevitable hopelessness of the situation.

West Street in which the great piano factory of Julius Bluethner had stood, looked as if two giant bulldozers had rolled from one end to another, reaching from Frankfurter-strasse to the new *Rathaus* (Martin Luther Ring). On both sides the fronts of the buildings had been completely scythed away. The backs of the buildings still stood and, as we climbed the back stairs of one of them, we found some acquaintances wearily sitting at a table in the kitchen with everything in chaos around them. Had they opened the door into the bed-rooms and living rooms, they would have stepped out into nothing.

Rescue workers were everywhere. I saw one wee boy of about four years old taken from what had once been a cellar. All his folk inside were dead from the blast. He had lived alone in that horror for hours. They gave him a bar of choco-late but he didn't even know where his mouth was any more.

Here and there faint cries came from below the earth, but it was questionable whether the rescuers could get the people out in time. No one knew where to start – the missing, the buried, the dead, were too many. There was no heavy machin-ery available and tools were far too few. In most cases the res-cuers worked with bare hands. Some who had been buried were lucky, others died of suffocation. Some of the dead were even luckier, they must have died instantly and never known the agony of the consequences of that night.

Added to the difficulties in rescue work were falling walls. There seemed to be continuous rumbling as now insecure bricks heaved outwards and tumbled with a horrifying roar to make the chaos even more chaotic. We were told that one twelve-year-old boy had a miraculous escape. He had been blasted from the window of his bedroom, still tucked in his bed, carried over the roofs of the houses opposite and, still in his bed, landed in the street on the other side. I wondered if it were true and if so if his parents had escaped too, and what had become of all his loved ones. Most escapes were not escapes from tragedy.

We returned, sadly, wearily, worn out with walking and even more exhausted with what we had seen, back to our children. When they cried that they were hungry we fed them what we had, apathetically. There was no milk for the little ones, for there was no transportation of any kind. All we had was what was already on our own kitchen shelves, which wasn't much, due to the rationing process. We were lucky that we had running water in our small area.

No one dared cook because of the danger of fire. The mains were broken and sewers smashed. It was not until four days later that we aroused from our stupor. There were no exceptions to the mental state we were all in. Only then did we realise that, apart from the children, not one of us had washed or eaten in all that time. It was as if we had been turned to stone, all we could do was stand about and stare at the empty horror. Gradually though, we came to life, and a few days later the word came that all women and children were to be evacuated.

11

About a week after the air raid which literally demolished the centre of Leipzig and a good deal of the outer limits, during December 1943, we were told to report to the school in our area at an early hour.

I spent the night packing everything I could into cases and trunks and into the pram. I was quite determined that if I had to evacuate then I would make a clean break of it, with no intention of returning. I even unscrewed the rockers from Michael's small rocking horse and then manipulated them, with the horse, into the pram, plus the awning. Had I known that for the next two weeks I would get next to no sleep, I would probably have tried to snatch a few hours' rest, but time was pressing and I didn't do so.

In the morning everything was ready. It is true there were many articles I had to leave behind, but the urgency of the situation dulled any sense of sentiment over the loss of material things. Here the main consideration was clothing, particularly for the children, and absolute necessities. Why I considered the rocking horse a necessity I will never know.

As a last thought as I left the room, I turned to look around for the last time and noticed my practically new curtains. There was no time for finesse, I grabbed the bottoms of each and yanked them down, stuffing them in on either side of the pram to ease the pressure of the rockers. A year later they were to come in handy as I made them into dresses.

Herr Baier, Frau Lässig's other lodger, helped me to carry my luggage to the school. It was an ambitious load and the wonder is that I got it all intact when I finally arrived at my destination in the south of Germany.

I carried Christopher, for there was no room for him in the

103

pram, and Michael trotted alongside. At the school we were loaded onto trucks with our belongings and driven to the Leipzig *Hauptbahnhof*. The devastation round this huge station, reputedly one of the largest in the world, was complete. The cellars beneath the station had been flooded. A bomb had struck in front of the station with such force and at such an angle that it had penetrated the 'invulnerable' cellars, breaking a water main as it went.

A train was already standing in the station and presumably any damage to the rails had been temporarily repaired as our evacuation seemed to be a priority. Family after family, we were loaded onto it. When it steamed out, no one knew where it was headed. The strange thing was that there was no speculation among the women as to where we were being taken, they didn't appear to care and were only anxious to get away from the devastation. In any case, the majority of them had lost most of their possessions in that last awful raid.

Progress was intermittent and it took several hours. We were unloaded at Grossenhain station, not far from Dresden. The platform was packed with women and children and luggage. Most of the children were subdued, even the more lively of them in normal times remained close to mothers' sides. This was fortunate because some of the women had four or five little ones to cope with. One woman, who everybody had considered blessed, had a brood of seven, all under ten years, calling for a major feat of control. Loudspeakers soon informed us of what we were to do. All our luggage was to be left on the platform and we were to proceed to a nearby inn and wait for instructions.

Boys from the Hitler Jugend 'Pimpfs', the junior branch, led the way and settled us at tables. We sat there all afternoon until it was dark while names were read out. As each name was called, a Pimpf walked up, took a piece of paper from the official's hand, glanced around until he saw the family indicated and then proceeded to usher them from the room.

At last it was our turn. We were led out into the darkness. It was freezing cold and keeping my balance on the icy road with a bulkily wrapped up baby on one arm while leading a small boy by the hand was almost impossible. Then, from somewhere the Pimpf allocated to us produced a toboggan on which he proceeded to tie Christopher; pulling it by a string, he led the way through the darkened streets of the town. Michael and I trudged along behind. Gradually the houses began to grow fewer, with considerable distances between them. Michael began to lag. He was, after all, only two years old. We must have walked three miles, with me carrying him for most of the distance, before we arrived at a farmhouse. The Pimpf knocked at the door and a man opened it.

'What do you want?' he asked belligerently.

The Pimpf told him. The farmer was expected to give us a room and bed until further notice. The man protested but, when I insisted we could not walk any further at that time of night, he relented and let us in. He led us through a huge kitchen with a stone floor and opened a door onto a tiny parlour leading off it. It was the coldest room it had ever been my experience to occupy.

I put the children to sleep on an overstuffed, hard horsehair sofa, still dressed in all their clothes, and covered them with rugs I had brought with me. Then I sat and shivered by their side all night. In the morning the farmer and his wife told me that we might occupy their parlour for a few days, but that in the meantime we should look for somewhere else to stay as they had no room.

I don't think they were deliberately unkind. Strangers, and particularly children, would have disrupted their farm work. It was just inconvenient and I think that probably in other circumstances they would have offered their home willingly to any family left homeless. But they, along with the rest of the townspeople and farmers, acted grudgingly because they had no option. The order was to billet so many and they had no redress.

The next day we walked back to the town and discovered that some of the families had found no place at all and had been lodged in the basement of the Pestalozi School. After speaking to one or two of the other women, some of whom had been through the same experience as we had, I decided to move my things to this school. At least it was warm.

The cellars in the school were a masterpiece. They were fitted out with double bunk beds, showers and everything necessary to live, except the means of making meals. The cooking was to be done by women's organisations elsewhere in the town and the food brought in to us. I found two vacant bunks and settled in.

When that was done, I proceeded to carry our luggage from the station (where it had remained overnight on the platform) to the school. But no amount of searching revealed my week-end case and in this I had packed every stitch of the boys' warm clothing and Christopher's nappies, thinking that I could keep this with me as it was reasonably easy to carry.

I reported the loss to the police and they promised to make a search. In the meantime I was directed to a women's organisation, where the boys were fitted out with a change of underclothing and I was given a few nappies. Obviously these were of the cloth type that needed washing each time, for there was no such thing in those days as the convenient disposable type.

Where the police found the case I don't know, but four days later it was dumped at the school with no explanation. Housed in this basement at the school there were about forty-three women, old men and children; and after the first two days no one seemed to be making any effort to find lodgings for us. Also, to make matters worse, the women ceased to bring in any food. No doubt their supplies had run out.

The cooks, who at first had been all eagerness, announced they could not cook any longer, for the number of refugees was far greater than their supplies. The few restaurants in this small town were more than useless to our purpose, for even in normal times there was little call for complete meals and in most cases they were geared only to cater to Sunday afternoon customers and served indifferent coffee and, rarely, in these days, cake. And, of course, in addition, our food coupons could not have stretched to daily meals outside our homes.

By great good luck I had brought with me, at Frau Lässig's suggestion, bearing in mind that I might find difficulty in heating the baby's bottle, a small electric plate and a very small saucepan. In the gymnasium of the school I found an electric outlet and there we queued, all forty-three of us, and in turn we cooked semolina in water in that one saucepan for the children. Semolina was only obtainable on children's ration cards and that at least we had managed to get. As the last one finished, so it would be time for the first one to begin again. It was quite a feat, but it worked.

After a few days of these makeshift conditions, my saucepan was in such a poor state that I had to throw it away, when we were told that more refugees were coming in and that we would have to be moved. Most of us were sent to another village, where we were dumped in the one and only village inn. From here we were again sent to various farmhouses. I was taken to a farm and housed. True, the farmer and his wife were not very willing, but they seemed to be making the most of a bad job and took us in on sufferance. Probably the village mayor was more strict than the one overlooking the previous village.

The room to which we were allocated had the luxury of a rather lumpy single bed in it, which was an improvement. The village itself was very small and there were no restaurants or shops at all. Once a week the baker, the butcher and the grocer called for orders. However, as these tradesmen had already made their weekly call the day before, I was told I could buy my food from the farm.

Now I began to understand why they were prepared to put up with us. They were practically self-supporting, and therefore were quite ready to earn an extra penny by charging and over-charging for everything we ate or even looked at. The room we were given was warm, though, and as the children were still so small, we all fitted in quite comfortably in the bed provided.

However, any money we had was quickly dwindling and so far there had been no indication as to how the transfer of military or family allowances was to be made. I decided, therefore, that as my pocket could not keep up with this extortion, we would be better off if I could get the children to Steisslingen.

107

Movement of civilians was now so restricted that before one could travel, a permit had to be obtained from the mayor of any town or village in order to get a ticket on the infrequent trains. The day before Christmas Eve I applied for a permit to travel and in this case the mayor was only too glad to find that at least one of the refugee families could be dropped from his responsibilities and gave permission gladly.

I then bribed a French prisoner-of-war who was working on the farm to take us on a cart back to Grossenhain station. We loaded our luggage and set off and were lucky enough to be able to get on a train heading, or so I hoped, in the right direction.

In actual fact, we reached Singen by means of several trains. The first one took us to Dresden. Here, I decided that in spite of the risk of losing a suitcase or two, it would be impossible to proceed hampered by so much luggage. Thinking back, I must have been crazy to have even attempted to take so much luggage. One case had been left in Grossenhain as the train steamed out. I had seen it standing on the platform as the train left and I gave this up for lost, for I knew there was only my name on the label and no address. Even had there been, it was, I felt, almost certain that with the disorganisation which was growing daily, it would be irretrievable.

A milling crowd of people filled the Dresden station, and everywhere there were enthusiastic uniformed Pimpfs dashing about on various errands. These young boys were to be commended for the part they played in helping civilians; honest, ever-ready and willing, they would have done justice to the Boy Scout movement.

I handed one of them a high-value Reichmark bill and asked him if he could register my luggage through to Singen. In no time at all he had the luggage labelled, stamped and then wheeled away for transport. I hoped, with not much faith, that it would eventually arrive at Singen.

After a short while the boy returned with the exact change for my money and then refused any payment for himself. The next train took us to Nürnberg, where we remained all night in the station while bombs fell all around. Here again, the

108

facilities for mother and child were excellent and as we waited we were made as comfortable as possible.

A train took us to Stuttgart and then another slow train wound its way through the ice and snow to Rottweil and eventually to Singen.

12

My experiences after the bombing of Leipzig seemed to last a million years. Physically and mentally, all my energies were exhausted, leaving only an urgent will to survive with the children. I have always felt that had I not had the children to bring to safety, I alone would never have survived.

Great-grandfather's farm was not large. The house where we lived was in the village, but the fields he owned were scattered at varying distances.

In this part of Germany such farms entailed hard work by the whole family to keep pace with the seasons. No one was excused. Even great-grandmother, when the necessity arose, manned a rake in the hayfields. The heavy burden of manual labour showed in the early aging of men and women; more perhaps in the women for, in addition, they had cooking, house-cleaning and the bearing and tending of the children.

When my mother-in-law was at home, she too was not exempt from field and housework, but she was frequently away visiting friends and relatives in other parts of the country. It was natural, therefore, that great-grandmother should care for the children and that I, so much younger, should take on any heavy work, in or out of the house.

Physically, I had little stamina. I had never weighed more than ninety-eight pounds, and now I was even less than that, so I discovered that my mind had to work where my body would have failed. Sheer doggedness pulled the rake or lifted sacks that were heavier than I was. My small hands and weak wrists were motivated by willpower, rather than muscle-power. Each day had to be dealt with as it came along. Each sack lifted without thought to the next. Each wind-row of hay raked before the next could be thought of. It was rather like aiming at a close target, knowing it would move back in the second before I hit gold.

And it wasn't only the work in the fields. It was getting into the fields which drained energy before I started. The roads were rutted and stony and my shoes thin. Walking was a misery and if, as was often the case, the fields were too far away to walk to, then we used a bicycle, and the ride was a penance.

The sun blazed down on the fields and the sweat dripped as we worked, attracting great horseflies, which clustered in black clots on the hides of the cows that pulled the haycarts and buzzed around us continuously, rising from us in clouds when we raised a weary arm to brush them off.

Dog-tired by evening, we trudged or rode home to our acid meal of black bread, sour cider and onion. Only on the very rare occasion was there the welcome addition of a hard-boiled egg or a piece of smoked sausage. Then there was washing to be done, fruit or vegetables to be preserved, milk to be taken to the dairy, eggs to be collected and delivered to the collection centres and the stables to be cleaned.

I might add here that only great-grandfather and great-grandmother, being the resident farmers, were allowed to keep sufficient milk, butter and eggs for their own use. All other such produce had to be taken to the dairy, where it was distributed. Certainly every farmer manipulated the proceeds of his farm, but there wasn't much room for over-indulgence as failure to comply with regulations exacted certain punishment in the form of even more restrictive allowances.

Fieldwork wasn't all, either. In their season, wild strawberries had to be picked for bottling, wild raspberries culled from nettle-infested slopes, the vegetable garden tended behind the house, and wood collected for burning in the great stove in which the bread was baked. This latter had its own hazards. Returning from the woods, hot, thirsty, dirty and tired, there still remained a disgusting task, we had to strip off and pick bloated wood ticks from our skin where, with their heads buried in our flesh, we could literally see their bodies dilating with our own blood.

Every task in that time had its own particular misery, be it physical or mental; little wonder that I forgot how to sing, to smile or to play with my children. To this day when I look back I regret how little they, or I, had of recreation with each other. No time for play, only for existence.

On Saturday the house was cleaned from top to bottom. Then, we rode on bicycles to Singen to make any exchanges for food that we could; or one of us rode to the mill, about five miles distant, with a bag of grain which from time to time we secreted from our delivery quota. I enjoyed this errand in spite of the bumpy road, for it led through the forest and so was peaceful. It was rare to meet anyone; the only living thing being an occasional deer crossing the path, the swift passing of a bird overhead or the chatter of a disturbed squirrel. Those were my 'thinking' times when I could transport my mind to England and home.

When I rode to Singen I took the children with me, Christopher in a basket chair attached to the handlebars, Michael in a similar chair strapped on the carrier. I rode Carl's old bicycle with a bar which made it difficult to mount and dismount, but I bore the load gladly, for it was almost the only time I had alone with the children.

On Saturday evening we still hadn't finished work, for as I have previously noted, each farmer was responsible for cleaning part of the roadway in front of his house, which had to be thoroughly swept. And on Sundays there was no excuse for lying in bed, for everyone was expected to go to church. By Sunday afternoon, having eaten the only substantial meal of the week, there was washing up to do, after which one could rest. But not for long. This was the time utilised by those who had to do any business with the farmers, as it was the only time they could be guaranteed to be caught at home.

One dressed in one's best and sat waiting for callers, when the time would have been better utilised in recuperating to be ready for the following week's work. The sheer drudgery of living at all sapped strength and in time destroyed any sense of humour. There wasn't one second of my waking hours when I didn't have to pressure my mind into trying to think out the situation. Any rumour, however fragile, I grasped at and built into strong reasons for the war ending and for our return to England. I fantasised on this one theme continuously.

At night I was, more often than not, too tired to sleep and then came the horror imaginings, for it was then that the planes flew over and we listened. Each change in the drone of engines brought us to the window to look upwards. But the planes were not the worst for me, worse still was waiting for a fist to hammer on the door. One heard 'things', rumours of atrocities, rumours of what was going on in concentration camps. Rarely did anyone know anything first-hand, yet fear mounted to unbelievable proportions. It ran like wildfire throughout the population. So bad was it, that we kept a pistol near the bed, determined to use it at the least sign that anything might happen which would drag us from the children, or the children from us. I used to pray and bite into my pillow with the mental agony of fear, desperately planning what to do if these fears became reality. And again, in an effort to shut out those terrible thoughts, night after night I'd force my thoughts back to England.

Often it wasn't until early morning that I fell asleep from exhaustion. Then, more often than not, I dreamed of walking down our road in England, past each neighbour's house, until the final luxury of opening the door of my parents' home and stepping to the doorstep to safety. The dream became an obsession, so that during the day as I worked, I would recall it, summoning up small details, trying to remember the layouts of individual gardens, paintwork, curtains, holding conversations with neighbours and friends, in fact anything to enhance my memories and to give me hope. But I never could get myself to believe it would ever really happen, it was all too remote and I could also never get beyond the door on my old home.

Night after night I played this game of make-believe either waking or dreaming; day after day was the same heavy farm work, hundredweight sacks of potatoes and apples to lift, scrubbing and raking, cleaning and polishing.

And no affection or kind words; even the short and rare times with my two babies was too brief, for great-grandmother was always present, taking precedence over any decisions regarding the boys. I had no say in the way they were brought up and waged a perpetual war with her in the preparation of Christopher's formula, to which she always added large quantities of butter and sugar. In consequences, the poor little fellow got so fat that I despaired for him.

Great-grandfather too was a problem, for he was so proud of Michael that he often gave him errands about which he could brag to his fellow farmers, but which made my heart leap into my throat for fear. On one occasion I saw the small lad toddling along pulling the big scythe behind him; at least he was trying to pull it until I snatched it from his hand. When I reproached great-grandfather, his only response was, 'Ah! Wah! He can do it, he is a strong boy.' And one day I caught him offering his glass of schnapps to Michael, who sipped, went red in the face and then to my horror drank a big gulp of it, much to great-grandfather's amusement. 'There you are, he's a man,' he bragged.

There were also other chores too. Each cellar had to be reinforced. This necessitated cutting trees, carrying them downstairs, and wedging them between the floor and ceiling. There was very little room in the cellar under the farmhouse in any case the walls were lined with rows of preserves in jars, bottled meat (the meat being our own rations), vegetables and fruit put down by my mother-in-law and ear-marked, as she constantly reminded, for use when Carl returned from the front. And, as I have already described, one corner was occupied by the enormous barrel for making schnapps. We didn't drink the schnapps, however; great-grandfather liked his glass at each meal, but the main purpose of it was exchange. A bottle of schnapps could purchase us butter, meat, or clothing and was invaluable.

It was in this small cellar that we sat when planes flew over, cramped together on the cellar steps or on the dirt floor until it was safe to emerge again.

13

That winter of 1943 was particularly cold. But despite the hazards of the weather, Russian girls who worked in the aluminium factory in Singen, either in pairs or singly, battled their way through deep snow to the countryside, begging for food from the farmers.

Because of the language difficulty, it was impossible to know exactly from where they had come, or why. We may, of course, have been quite wrong in our interpretation of the few words and many signs with which they attempted to make themselves understood. It seemed, however, that they had been transported from Russia in order to work in the factories in Germany, which had for some time been suffering from a shortage of labour. Certainly they had not come willingly. Some were educated students, some were peasants, but one thing they all had in common ... their bare feet.

They were gentle, kind and strong and they looked in horror at the heavy work my mother-in-law set me to do. I suppose this was because I was so much more fragile in build than they. If my mother-in-law was out of the way, it was not unusual for a couple of these girls to take me by the arms and forcibly seat me in a chair while they set to with their muscular heavy bodies to scrub the floors, and they certainly made a better job of it than I ever could.

After a while, we thought we might ease their situation a bit by helping them with clothing. The garments they wore were shapeless and drab. They all wore the traditional head shawl covering their hair and more often than not they wore bulky men's jackets and long skirts. Their clothing gave forth a metallic smell from their constant proximity with the aluminium factory. We found that they had little or no underclothing and so we tore up old sheets and sewed them into necessities for warmth. We also made blouses for them. One girl whom we called 'schöne Maria' (beautiful Maria), to distinguish her from her friend, who was also called Maria and who was excessively plain-featured, came to us one day and asked us if we would make her a '*Hanf*'. This floored us. After long consideration we decided that the girl needed a maternity dress. From the shape of her it certainly seemed the logical conclusion.

We waved our hands to demonstrate – we patted her and eventually drew a picture of a tent-like dress. It was no good. Each time she shook her head and said '*Hanf*'. In the end we undid her jacket and found that underneath was not only another jacket but a flour sack wrapped around her for warmth.

Then, and then only, did we realise that what she wanted was a *Hemd* (shirt). She had heard the German word for that article and presumed that the word for a blouse was the same. Underneath all the padding she was as slender as a reed, which was quite unusual for most of these girls had quite sturdy, squat bodies. They had terrific stamina and were capable of carrying a load that might have been a problem for the average man.

Quite close to the aluminium factory was a Russian prisoner-of-war camp, and we found that the girls came out to the villages not only to fetch food for themselves, but to get bread and potatoes to supplement the food for their countrymen. This service received a sad lack of reward later when the men were freed at the end of hostilities.

The loaded sacks with which they returned to Singen, the greater part of which contained potatoes and swedes, must often have weighed close to half a hundredweight.

Then they began to bring out toys made from aluminium foil of all different colours. They gave scraps which were too small for use in the factory to the Russian prisoners-of-war, who made the toys in their spare time. Many of these playthings were quite ingenious and surprisingly sturdy. Carousels with horses and riders which actually moved, birds which flew on sticks, butterflies, clowns ... all were perfectly made and the payment asked was food.

I can remember the girls asking Michael what he would like to have. I say 'they asked' because strangely enough, although we adults found it so difficult to understand them (for during their stay in the area the girls picked up only a very few words of German), Michael seemed to understand them and they in turn understood his childish prattle.

He promptly told them that he wanted a toy plough. No amount of alternative suggestions would shake him ... a plough it must be. A week later the plough was produced: standing on an eighteen-inch long board, complete with farmer and four horses to pull it, each about six inches high, everything perfectly proportioned. They hadn't forgotten Christopher either, who received a working model of a carousel with six brightly coloured horses.

All this time there had been Polish prisoners-of-war in an old farmhouse in the village. They were considered 'safe' and were set to work helping the farmers. As with the French prisoners the year before, they came to our house through the back way after dark and studied maps; not for escape purposes but to follow the progress of the war.

Here in Steisslingen, it was reasonably easy for me to listen to the radio from England. I say easy, because in this respect my mother-in-law and her parents hated the Nazi regime. But the utmost care had to be observed while listening. Our chairs had to be pulled quite close to the loudspeaker, which was, of necessity, tuned as low as possible.

I was, of course, the only one who understood English and I translated for my mother-in-law. Great-grandmother on the other hand was not so interested in the news as in the reporter's voice, which fascinated her, and she loved to hear Big Ben chiming the hours. One of its bells was cracked and when is sounded, she beamed happily, saying with satisfaction, 'There now! Did you hear it? It clappered.'

We also listened to the Swiss stations whenever possible so that my mother-in-law could understand the language. Now and again we had narrow escapes. One Sunday afternoon in particular we left the dial switched to Swiss Beromuster. Music followed the news and we were talking, quite forgetting to switch back to the German channel. This music therefore was an unnoticed background to our conversation and because of our talking we failed to remember whence the music was coming.

Suddenly the door to the parlour opened and in walked the Party leader of the village – Herr Baumann. It was not unusual for people to walk in unannounced and we really should have been more cautious, for in these little villages it was rare for house doors to be locked or closed. Even at night, except in bitter weather, the doors usually stood open for anyone to enter.

Herr Baumann was selling *Winterhilfszeichen*. These were little souvenirs, sold each month for the assistance of the poor, and there were some very pretty and also interesting examples among them. One month a whole series of wildflower pictures could be bought, another it was tiny wooden figures, pieces of amber, birds or animals. What they were on this occasion I can't remember, for to my horror the music suddenly stopped and a voice announced 'Here is Swiss Beromunster.'

I saw my mother-in-law tense, and then she started talking earnestly and quickly to Baumann while I slowly backed to the instrument and turned the knob, praying as I did so that the next point on the dial would also be music, so that the difference would not be too obvious.

It seemed he hadn't noticed, but even so we couldn't be sure; for days we didn't touch the radio at all and lived in expectation of repercussions.

On another evening, while listening rather late, with my ear pressed against the radio, which was very softly tuned in, there was a terrific bang on the closed shutters over the windows. We never did find out whether someone was in actual fact giving us a warning or whether someone had thrown a snowball. But whatever it was, for days after we were again afraid of repercussions.

The Poles, who were always anxious to know the news, usually dropped in during the evening to ask what the situa-

118

tion was; and one of them, Andreas, was always welcome. He was a gentle, quiet man. He had seen his wife and children killed in Poland after the beginning of hostilities, at the same time as he himself was taken prisoner and removed to work in Germany. He asked nothing more of life than a kindly word and the privilege of being allowed to look at my two boys while they were sleeping.

We had problems with great-grandfather too. More often than not when he asked us about the news to which we were illicitly listening, we pretended we hadn't heard him. This would anger him and he would thump on the table and shout at us to give him an answer. If we said we did not know or couldn't remember, he would wheedle and question us until eventually in desperation we told him. A few minutes later, and this happened all the time, we would see him across the road at the farm opposite passing on what we had told him to his friends. It never failed.

The fact that some of the farmers thereabouts were in fear of the Government and wanted the Allies to win was of little comfort to us; for there were others in the village, such as Baumann, who had very long ears. Any false move could prove fatal.

We usually had some idea who was of the same opinion as ourselves, but it was quite another thing to voice those opinions openly. It was therefore very important to forestall great-grandfather before he got to his friends or, if he eluded us long enough to actually get to them, to find some reason to call him back to the house.

Each time we explained the dire consequences of letting *anyone* know that we had heard the news. But to all this he always answered with an 'Ah-wa-wa – who cares, no one likes Hitler anyway.' He could not, or would not, understand the danger he was putting us in with his enthusiasm for even minor victories of the 'other side'.

Michael too was a potential danger, for Baumann's father lived next door to us. His little grand-daughter Gerda, who was a playmate of Michael's, also lived there; and while we were careful of what we said in front of our tiny boy, there was always the danger that he would repeat some of the things the old folk said, and none of those bits he picked up were ever very flattering to the Führer.

14

A year had gone by sadly since we had left Leipzig; now, nearly every day, planes flew in over the village from the direction of Switzerland. It was as if there were an air 'street' above us and the planes looked like silver birds. Predatory silver birds.

The only fear we had from them was that they might develop engine trouble which would force one of them to drop its load in order to escape back over the Swiss frontier and then to Britain. It was, of course, forbidden to fly over Switzerland, it being a neutral country, but there were many humorous stories told about this. One of them was that the Swiss radioed a British plane flying over...

'You are flying over Swiss territory.'

'We know.'

'If you don't turn back we must fire on you.'

'We know.'

The Swiss then fired their anti-aircraft guns and the occupants of the plane radioed, 'You are aiming too high.'

'We know,' the Swiss replied.

Another story was that when the Allies were bombing Friedrichshafen on the other side of Lake Constance, the Swiss turned their searchlights full on to the site being bombed.

Whether these stories were true or not was never established, but we drew comfort from the fact that if they were, the results would contribute to a swifter ending of our misery.

There were very few air raids near our village, but on Christmas Eve 1944 a number of planes flew in and bombed Singen. For once in our village, we heard the warning sirens as the wind was blowing in our direction.

From the distance we could hear the thudding of the bombs

and see the columns of smoke. Later, when we bicycled down to the town, we saw the tragedy of houses partly demolished. Many of them had Christmas trees standing in their wrecked, abandoned rooms. These poor remnants of tinsel, ornaments, gingerbread and a few poor presents, forlorn and disregarded, were even more saddening to see at this time, for even if the givers and the recipients were not dead or injured, we could visualise the agony of those who had lost their homes at what should have been a peaceful and happy time of year.

With time, however, we developed a sentimental regard for one aeroplane. At least we always thought of it as being the same plane... At night, as it circled the district, we were not afraid of it, for we knew it was a reconnaissance plane, watching the railway stations in the district around us. We in our small village could boast no railway station, nor wanted to. When referring to this plane it was always as '*Bahnhof* Charlie' (Station Charlie). It was quite a comforting feeling when we heard his engines, for we knew while he was flying around, no attackers would fly in to disturb us.

One day we had an air raid alarm during the afternoon. Michael was at the time playing in a carpenter's shed just up the road with two other small boys. At the first sound of the siren I rushed as quickly as I could go towards the shed, for I had no wish to see again the sight of a small boy running wildly on short fat legs up the road, screaming for fright, as he had done once before when hearing an aeroplane in Leipzig. The sound had brought back memories of that night of chaos there.

I was not in time to prevent a small panic, however, as the three boys strove simultaneously to burst out of the door of the shed. It was then that I realised how essential it is for safety that doors should open outward – and this particular door opened inward. In their fright their instinct was to push, and they found themselves trapped inside, with all of them screaming with fright.

However, having got Michael home, he soon forgot and played happily through the rest of the alarm with a neighbourhood child, Gisela. When the 'all clear' sounded I took her hand to take her home. But, in these small towns 'all clears' and alarms often took their cue from unreliable sources, with not too accurate results; at the end of the road which led onto the main Singen–Stockach road, we saw an aeroplane coming straight up, over the length of the street.

It was flying low and machine-gunning as it came. It was so low that I could see the faces in the cockpit. There was only one thing to do, press Gisela against the wall of a barn under the overhanging eaves and stand over her until he had flown by. The child was speechless with fright, and I was little better, as we dodged from cover to cover until we reached her home ... for we couldn't know if other stray planes still had to fly back to the safety of the frontier, and we knew if they did they were bound to fly over us.

15

One night I awoke to hear aeroplanes overhead. This time it was not our comforting *Bahnhof* Charlie, and I had an instinctive feeling that something would go wrong. I dressed the boys and myself quickly, and tried to persuade my mother-in-law to get up. A woman of many moods, she was just going through one of not caring what happened to her – at least so she said.

'Why bother? My boy is at the front, what do I have to live for?'

That was the remark most frequently on her lips the past few days. The mood was not likely to exist long, she was just as likely to suddenly decide to go away for a few days to thoroughly enjoy herself with relatives, supposedly wealthy, but whom I never met and whose name I never knew.

The same moods governed her when she had several of her husband's suits made over into costumes for herself; as, according to her, it was a waste for them to hang for the moths to get at. Having few clothing points myself and having made over many of my own clothes for the boys, most of which I had brought with me from England, I suggested tentatively that I should do the same with one of Carl's suits. This was different. In this case I was heartless.

'How could you consider,' she said vehemently, 'changing any part of what belonged to Carl, and what would he do when he got back for clothes?'

So, on this occasion it took a lot of persuasion to get her grudgingly from her bed and starting to dress herself. Then, before she was fully clothed, there was a frightful roar. It sounded as if the noise was coming from under the roof. I picked up the boys and threw them onto the sofa and myself on top of them, as the house shook with a deafening explosion which rocked the village. As the noise subsided I left the boys where they were and rushed to the stairs and up them two at a time, feeling as I did so a rush of hot air playing on my legs through the floorboards. Running into the greats' bedroom, I dragged the old people out of bed, thrusting their clothes into their hands, and then pushed them to the door.

'Get downstairs, it doesn't matter what you look like,' I yelled in their bewildered, sleepy, questioning faces. And then, for no reason that I could think of, I took a huge picture of their eldest son Carl, who had been killed in the First World War, pulled it from the hook on the wall and staggered after them, clutching in my hands the heavy gilt-framed two-and-a-half-foot-wide memento.

I think this was the only time I was unpractical during the war and I suppose was on a par with the stories one heard about people rushing back into homes, grabbing a kitchen drawer full of string and bits and pieces and leaving their valuables or clothing to burn.

Leaving the old people with the boys in the parlour, I went to the front door and saw in the middle of the road a crowd of gesticulating neighbours ... and my mother-in-law completely unnoticed by those around her, clad in her brassiere and panties. It was cold too, for snow was on the ground, but I don't think she even noticed the weather or her unclothed state, the shock of the explosion had been so great.

About one hundred yards up the road, towards the small lake, there was a red glow as the perishable parts of an aeroplane went up in flames.

There was no more sleep that night. Everybody had a different version of the event; it was not until the next morning that the priest, Pfarrer Stroebel, told us what really happened. He, as usual when there was any sign of trouble, had run to the door of his church. From there he had a good view of the surrounding countryside as the church was situated on a hill in the centre of the village. He had seen the plane flying over, heard the engines miss, and watched it as it turned, apparently in an attempt to get back over the Swiss border.

Twice, he said, as it seemed inevitable that it would fall into the village, he had seen it take a sharp turn upwards, only to fall again, crashing just a few yards beyond the limit of the houses.

He told us more, too; he had seen several parachutes descending at intervals, and finally just before the plane nose-dived to earth, a last parachute had been seen slowly drifting down. He had run in the direction in which it appeared to be falling, and in the school yard had found the pilot, a Canadian, stunned by his landing but otherwise unharmed. Wrapped round his wrist and held firmly in one hand was his rosary.

Before the authorities arrived, Father Stroebel had heard that this pilot had on some previous occasion passed through the district and had remembered the village. Twice on this night he had attempted to steer his machine up and away from the houses. Ordering his crew to bale out, he had remained with it until it was safely near the lake before he too had jumped for safety.

With the first light of day we walked over to the wreckage. The sun was shining and gave the scene a Christmassy effect, for the top of the deep snow was covered with the aluminium foil used for radar purposes. We, of course, didn't know its purpose and there was much speculation as to what it might be.

In the midst of this sparkling landscape lay the plane, broken and burned. I searched around the wreckage, but apart from pieces of the actual plane, the only thing I found was a burned glove which I took home with me. Later in the morning I walked over to the plane again with other sightseers, but this time the wreckage was surrounded by a guard of SS troops brought in for duty from the Radolfzell Barracks.

A query as to what had been done with the pilot and the rest of the crew elicited the reply that they were being housed temporarily in the prisoner-of-war house opposite the village hall.

Perhaps because we were living in a quieter area reasonably far away from any town, where there was much more Party activity, restrictions didn't weigh so heavily on us. Or perhaps any restrictions, apart from those on commodities, seemed unreal to us. There was also the fact that although Baumann and his cohorts were constantly seen strutting about in their Party uniforms, they had been born and raised in the village and had been to school with many of the farmers, who were, as a consequence, quite unable to take him really seriously, even though they realised that he could be dangerous.

Whatever the reason, while we were all wary of what we said and to whom we spoke, when anything of consequence happened, such as this aeroplane crashing in our immediate neighbourhood, the villagers' reaction was a normal one of inquisitiveness and interest, rather than caution.

Our reactions to the plane crash could be construed, I suppose, as unwise, yet throughout the war people were doing things which were not only unwise but downright foolhardy in an effort to help a cause or to alleviate the suffering of others.

When we heard the plane was Canadian, the reaction was to see if anyone was alive and, if so, could they be helped. As far as I was concerned a Canadian spoke English, and this was the nearest I was to get in a long, long time to the comfort of my mother tongue.

So, well aware that we were daring the devil, a group of us walked out to the scene of the crash again, found we couldn't get near and turned back at the sight of the guard now in formation around the wreck.

Herr Oexele, the village *Bürgermeister*, owned the grocery store next to our house. He was friendly, and although he never spoke of it, the blind eye he turned on some actions and remarks made in the village could be construed to mean that he too, in spite of his position, was anti-Hitler.

There seemed no harm to me, therefore, in going to the village hall and asking him about the crew. I thought that if I could get their names, or even the name of one of them, I could get in touch with their relatives after the war.

Thinking in those times and in the middle of the war arena wasn't as sane and sober as in peacetime. Drama, heroics, fantasies, beliefs and actions were all so much more magnified

127

that one hardly knew what activated one's actions. As well as this, more often than not any action had to be spontaneous, or not at all, with greater risks taken.

Unfortunately, when I tried to go in to speak to Herr Oexele, two individuals outside stopped me. Both were jackbooted officials (jackboots still have the effect of sending chills up my spine), I walked over and found myself standing in front of them, rather like a naughty schoolgirl, as they began to question me. And, what was worse, to my embarrassment a crowd began to gather to listen. Most of them were, I knew, sympathetic, because I was well acquainted with their view-points, but it was equally obvious that no one was going to spare me this embarrassment by missing a choice example of bullying.

I doubt even if I had been a man they would have lifted a finger to help, but in this part of the country, where a woman was held to be the inferior sex, they certainly weren't sympathetic enough to stick their necks out for me.

The two officials questioned me closely and discovered that my father was born in Germany and that my husband was at the front. They insisted that it followed as the night the day, that I was German and that my interest in a British crew (British? Canadian? It was all the same to them) could only be interpreted as traitorous.

The fact that many other villagers had been interested enough to go to the scene made no difference, I was to be the example. With my face brightly marked with the face-slapping which had punctuated the questioning, I left, scared to death. The consequences, I knew, could be disastrous, if not fatal.

I returned home and discovered that some 'kind soul' had offered the entirely false information that I was teaching the boys English. The boys' English at this time amounted to a 'Mummy' instead of a German '*Mutti*' and 'bunny' for a rab-bit. Apart from which, I certainly had no time from the farm work for teaching anything. Now I come to think of it, I won-der how this 'sin' on my part could be reconciled with their continued teaching of English in their schools.

A few minutes after I returned home, these men appeared

again, this time at our front door. Great-grandmother Xaveria, seeing them coming, snatched up the two boys. As small as she was, she ran, with one tucked firmly under each arm, into the woods at the back of the house and remained there with them until the men had left. After a great deal of stamping about and shouting and threats, they left, with the parting shot that I would certainly be brought to book.

I believed them. There was no reason not to, it had happened before, was indeed happening in thousands of homes every minute. The fact that I had always anticipated something of the sort didn't make the situation any easier. I was terrified.

Later in the day, two of the villagers came past and said that one of the crew of the plane had been picked up by an SS truck and that it would be driving past our house quite soon. By this time I was so overwrought with fear that it took some persuasion on my mother-in-law's part to get me to leave the house, but eventually I did so. Even then, I didn't think I would have enough courage to call out to the prisoner as the truck passed, as she wanted me to.

We watched as the truck came up over the hill and toward the house, but when I saw him, so young, so alone and guarded by these severe guards, my fear left me, and I called out, 'Keep your chin up, lad,' as he was driven by. I hope very much that the surprise of an obviously English accent gave him a boost.

We lived in suspense during the next two weeks for every minute of the day, and it was even worse at night. I expected to hear hammering on the door, and my thoughts would turn to nothing other than how I would get away with the children ... plus the even bigger problem ... where to?

Faced with the threat of losing them, not by death but by that which would be perhaps worse, their being taken away from me, my imagination ran riot.

Death, terrible as it is, in some cases when it strikes children leaves the parents in agony and loss. But the agony of mind of the parent or parents who have their children snatched away from them to the unknown, where they know them to be living, lost, frightened and calling for mother and father who can't answer them, is far, far worse.

Many a night I tossed with my unbearable thoughts, until I turned over and bit into the pillow at the prospect, not only of my fear, but even more of theirs.

Sure enough, the knock came; not, as we had anticipated in the night, but one afternoon. The front door was, as usual, open; as great-grandmother saw the uniformed official with his hand on the handle of the parlour door, she picked up the children and in a flash was gone.

What their young minds must have made of this peculiar grown-up kind of hide-and-seek I cannot guess. Nor, had the worst come to the worst, would Xaveria's temporary disappearance with them have helped, for they would speedily have been found.

The main thing, as we planned this move beforehand, was that they should be out of the way, in the hope that it would be 'out of sight, out of mind'.

There was, however, no gainsaying the sight of the extremely tall man in the SS uniform who marched in and announced that he 'had a bone to pick with me'. My mother-in-law followed us into the parlour but she was pushed from the room and the door closed in her face, so that I was alone with him.

What should I say to him? Should I explain? What was there to explain? Should I keep silent?

I decided perhaps it would be better to say nothing, for whatever I did say, I was convinced would be twisted to suit their purpose.

The officer took some papers from a briefcase and riffled through them slowly. I kept my eyes on his hands. Suddenly they were still, and he said 'Well?'

No answer.

'Tell me what happened.'

Still no answer, and in the silence, the ticking of the clock on the wall sounded louder and louder in my ears. Then he said in a quiet voice, 'Look at me.'

So quiet and so still was his voice that I slowly raised my eyes to his face. Then he said, 'I want you to believe me, you must believe me. I will try and help you.'

130

And indeed, when I looked into his kind and sad eyes, I realised that a miracle had happened.

I told him of the events surrounding the crashing of the plane, that there had been no harm in what I had done, that I was only interested in the occupants of the plane because perhaps at some time I might be able to let their families know what had happened to them. I told him about my being in Germany, about my boys, about everything. But I fully expected the miracle to dissolve at any moment and leave me in the middle of that ghastly nightmarish fear again.

But it didn't.

When I stopped talking, he said, 'Now I'll confide in you. It may make you less fearful for your future.'

He told me that he was a forester and game warden and that he had been drafted into this department. He told me how much he hated it, and all his longing for the clean forests and woodlands.

Then he took up the papers he had been handling and tore them up in front of me.

'I shall make a report,' he said. 'It will contain a complete explanation of my satisfaction that your actions had been misinterpreted. You will hear no more of this.'

With that he left.

I let an hour go by before I dared to go out. I felt sure that he had been honest with me, and yet there was still the lurking fear that perhaps I was imagining the miracle.

Still wondering, I ran to the *Bürgermeister*'s office in the village hall. Herr Oexele was not only the *Bürgermeister*, he was our neighbour and grocer. His house backed onto our yard and I knew he would tell me the truth.

'Have you seen him?' I stammered.

'Oh yes! The official, you mean.' He smiled. 'Yes, I've seen him. He walked in here and said that he had investigated the matter, that he was completely satisfied and that the case would be dismissed as unimportant.'

Again I was saved.

But fear does not disappear as easily as that, nightmares remain and always I expected the horror to be repeated. I was afraid to voice an opinion, to talk of anything but work and weather. I was wary and suspicious of everyone. I was always afraid, I could only trust the doctor and his wife.

16

Shortly after that a group known as the *Heckenschützen* (hedge fighters, or home protectors) was organised. This meant that every available man and boy was to be trained so that they could make a last stand against the enemy. Small trenches were dug in and about the villages and the whole group was actually a last hope. The Allies had, by this time, penetrated so far east that even the German radio conceded that they were on German soil, of course adding that this was part of their own strategy. At last the eternal dreariness of our immediate existence was changing. We hoped it forecast the end, and even timidly dared to speak about an end, amongst ourselves.

A meeting was held by Baumann, the Nazi official in the village, at the Gasthaus zur Krone. All available men and boys were called to this meeting.

Among these was a French officer. An Alsatian by birth, he had been called early in the war to the French flag, to which he had sworn allegiance. He never spoke of the events leading up to his being brought into Germany, so that I do not know if he was on leave at the time he was captured, or whether he was taken during the fighting in France. In any event, he had been brought to the village by the Germans as a teacher at the school since he was bilingual.

His wife came with him and he boarded in one of the farmhouses in the centre of the village. He was a pleasant person to speak to. His name was Jacques, but now I can neither remember his wife's name, nor their surname.

I do remember, however, that he made quite a name for himself in the village because of the fact that he was an expert knitter. He would have put most women to shame with his industry, executing the most intricate of Fairisle patterns in the pullovers he knitted for his wife and for some of the villagers who happened to have re-knittable wool. He was a quiet and well-liked man.

At this meeting he was told that he too must swear an oath of allegiance to the band of *Heckenschützen* but he took a firm stand and said that, as he had already taken the oath on the French flag, another would constitute a *Meineid* or perjury.

His wife was afraid of the consequences of his decision, and at her insistence they travelled to Constance to take advice of the Party officials there. They, in turn, confirmed what he had already averred. They told him to return home and that they would advise Baumann not to interfere with him or press him further in the matter.

He heard no more for about a week; then one evening as he was sitting knitting just before supper, the village gendarme knocked at the door and told him he was to go to the village hall. Not dreaming of any further difficulty, Jacques told his wife that he would be back within the hour and off he went, whistling down the street.

I had during the afternoon, as I recalled afterwards, seen *Bürgermeister* Oexele standing outside his little grocery store, which backed onto our farmhouse. He was very white of face and with him were Baumann and another man in uniform. Both were gesticulating as if they were having an argument. As it transpired they had been asking Oexele for the keys to the hall, and having been advised of their purpose, he was reluctant to part with them.

At 9.30 p.m. Jacques' wife came to our house to ask if we had seen anything of him. It was a windy, dark night and pouring with rain, but she was so obviously worried that I put on my raincoat and went out with her. As we approached the hall we saw three men standing outside, two of them in Party uniform; the other was the gendarme.

'Have you seen Jacques?' she asked. 'He said he would only be about an hour and he hasn't come back yet – his supper is getting cold.'

The answer stopped us in our tracks. It was so unexpected,

134

so horrible and yet even then we misunderstood what the gendarme said: 'You won't see him again, he has been shot.' That was what he actually said, but we both thought he said, 'He *will* be shot.' Neither of us stopped to ask questions ... we ran.

It wasn't true, it couldn't be true, we kept reassuring ourselves as we hurried to the home of the headmaster. He, as horrified as were we, hastily threw on a coat, saying that he would see what he could do.

Again we made our way to the village hall and, crossing the road, we could see the small main door standing open. All the windows were dark and the men had disappeared. Except for the wind, it was very quiet ... too quiet.

With the aid of a flashlight to guide us, we walked in and tried the offices on the ground floor. They were all closed and locked. From the main hallway a centre staircase divided to right and left halfway up to the first floor, where there were more offices. Presumably before the war these offices had been occupied by clerks, but during the war they were not used, as far as we knew, most of the business being done solely by the *Bürgermeister* himself.

'We had better go upstairs and look,' the headmaster said.

Slowly we ascended, but halfway up we halted. An ominous red trickle was running down the stairs. The door at the top immediately in front of us was closed, but it was clear that something was inside the room, for the red trickle was pooled on the landing.

'Go back,' the headmaster warned, as he turned the handle and pushed the door open. But by now the correct meaning of the gendarme's words was becoming clear in our minds and we pushed in behind him.

Jacques was dead.

He lay on the floor, riddled with bullets. But it was clear that his death had not been as simple as that. Turned over at the side of him was a cast-iron stove about three feet square and he was attached to it by ropes. Baumann and the other official had decided to go against the ruling of their superiors in Constance – they had tied him to the stove, which was

135

free-standing on a concrete base, then they had beaten him, possibly with the idea of softening him up and impressing him with the fact that he should not have gone over their heads. Who knows what their original ideas had been. So badly was he beaten that one eye was hanging loosely on his cheek. Blood was everywhere. It was also apparent that he had put up a desperate fight at some point, for pieces of Nazi uniform were scattered all over the room and it was Jacques who, in his struggles, had wrenched the stove off the base on which it stood. It was probably at this time that the men had decided that it had gone too far for a warning and had commenced shooting.

We took his wife, who was in a state of collapse, back to the headmaster's house. There was nothing we could do. Nothing we dared do. It was useless to ask questions. We didn't even dare move his body.

During the afternoon of the next day the gendarme called on Jacques' wife and told her to make arrangements to have her husband buried. Poor fellow, he also could not jeopardise himself by helping. All he dared do was to take orders and see that they were carried out. That was the tragedy we were all faced with. A one-man rebellion would have achieved nothing; for that matter, even the whole village united could have done nothing. One had too much to lose and so little to gain.

No one prevented the funeral. Funerals in this part of the world were quite different to any I had seen before. The village was, as I have said already, almost entirely Roman Catholic; before being carried to its last resting place the coffin, which for two days had rested open in the parlour of a bereaved family, was closed and carried out to trestles at the front door of the house. Candles were lit at the head and foot and a small vessel of Holy Water placed at the foot. Each villager, man, woman and child, then sprinkled a little onto the lid of the coffin as they passed by. The coffin was then lifted onto a cart drawn by two horses, the cart being piled high with wreaths and crosses, most of them home-made.

As it moved off, the priest walked behind it. Then came the men, headed by the nearest male relative. If the one who had died was survived by his wife, she could not take precedence over the men. Lining up in threes and fours, this long cavalcade of men then moved on and only when all had passed did the widow step forward and lead an equally long cavalcade of women. And, as they moved, one or other would commence praying and everyone would take up the chant until it became a loud incantation which could be heard quite a distance away. Thus they would walk to the cemetery, where the priest took over the burial service. For Jacques, a stranger to the village, the procedure was the same, except that possibly the cavalcade was longer.

The way to the cemetery was past Baumann's house and, as the procession passed, the murmur of voices grew louder. It appeared almost as if his house was unoccupied so still was it; but towards the end of the procession a curtain was seen to twitch and suddenly it was pulled aside, the window thrown open and in a loud voice Baumann could be heard shouting, 'You should all be shot in the feet.'

This statement was to backfire not too long after. It was some months later, when the French took over the village, that Jacques was taken from the alien earth in which he lay and with military honours transported back to his home in Alsace. Jacques' case was investigated and the day his body was exhumed, an army truck manned by French troops stopped at Baumann's door. He was given no time to put on his boots but was taken in his socks to the woods above the house. There they told him to run and then shot him down as he ran. His father was told to bury him outside the village.

After Jacques' death, it was difficult to know who was living in the greater suspense ... the Germans for fear of the French coming, or me for fear they would not get there quickly enough. Above all, it was becoming more and more difficult to keep Michael and great-grandfather quiet. Michael, a great chatterbox, as most children are, and who was often around when great-grandmother talked of her hate for the authorities, thought it great fun to repeat what she said at the most awkward times. Great-grandfather, as always, related the details to the neighbours whenever he had the chance and never in a quiet voice. We all lived in great excitement and anticipation now that the end was in sight, and his enthusiasm would be accompanied by arm waving and empathetic jubilation.

Another danger was the Serbian prisoners-of-war ... true they meant well and were always welcome at our house. They came late in the evenings, so, when they heard of any new victory on the part of the Allies and they shouted for joy, it called immediate attention to themselves and queries as to why the sudden happiness.

One day I heard that Belgrade had been recovered and as I walked down the village street on my way to a store, I passed a Serbian leading an ox-cart. I passed on the news to him, muttering it from the side of my mouth as he walked by me, for, of course, we were supposed to have no communication with the prisoners other than to do with the work they were doing.

This prisoner was so elated that he immediately let out a loud whoop and threw his hat into the air. All of this was of course under the watchful eye of Baumann and didn't pass without comment, for later in the day I was visited in great haste by the doctor, who advised me to lie low for a while as Baumann was suspicious and had vowed that I would be the next to come under his iron fist.

I was now quite certain that the French Army was not too far away and we made our plans accordingly. We decided that a British flag might help us when the village was taken. The materials were soon found: bright blue bed-ticking for St Andrew's cross; the red material was more difficult and it didn't appear we had anything the right colour until I remembered the Nazi flag. I unpicked one of these and, discarding the black swastika, found the red and the white exactly suitable to the purpose.

At one time I would never have dared to trust anyone, but now, as the end drew near, we began to discover more and more people with the same opinions as our own. This time I felt safe enough as I went into the tailor's little workroom with the materials tucked snugly at the bottom of my purse. While he snipped and stitched under my guidance, I sat and watched his machine whizzing up the seams. He actually turned out a perfect little flag, which I still have – not big but adequate, and we hid it for the time being under the kitchen cupboard.

The village had been fortified with tank defences which consisted of heavy tree trunks piled up and blocking the roadways entering and leaving the village. There was much discussion and head shaking as a result of these barricades. Everyone knew that if they were left standing, we would be bombarded from the air until they were removed. Iron fists, a most deadly type of grenade, had been stored close to each barrier.

Not long after these defences had been erected, a company of Indian soldiers entered the village. It was a little doubtful as to what their use was – that they were in German uniform was certain, but it was puzzling as Indians had been under British rule and should have been on the other side.

The first time I saw them was when a truck stopped opposite our farmhouse. I heard Michael crying and ran out to him. He was protesting at the manhandling of a sheep which appeared to be struggling to get away. Their treatment of the animal was so brutal that Michael was thoroughly upset. There appeared no way that I could stop them so I took the boy inside, at the same time expressing my disgust at these 'turncoats' as I felt them to be. But I didn't know the whole story.

The next day three of them knocked on our door and asked if the 'British lady' lived here. I answered coldly that I was from England and asked them what they wanted.

'Will you please make us a cup of tea?' asked one of them politely, holding out a packet of that commodity.

'Why?' I asked.

'Because no one else here could make a proper cup of tea,' he smiled.

'What are you doing in those uniforms then?' I retorted.

'That we can explain if you would be good enough to make the tea,' he insisted.

My mother-in-law at this point said they had better come in. While we watched for the kettle to boil they introduced themselves.

'I am Joseph,' said one, pointing to himself. 'He is Joseph

also,' he continued, pointing to the other, and then with scorn he said, 'that other is a Mohammedan and he will not drink with us, it is against his religion.'

Then he told us that they had been taken prisoner and placed in a camp.

'At first we were treated the same as the other prisoners,' said Joseph number one, 'but then, when the German soldiers became fewer in numbers, we were asked if we would fight for them. Naturally we refused.'

I raised my eyebrows and he continued, 'We didn't fall in with their request immediately, but our food supplies grew smaller and we were eventually told that if we didn't fight, our rations would be cut off altogether ... and here we are.'

They told us that they were to be used in defending the villages, and it appeared that was indeed their purpose, for immediately after they arrived they began to dig more ditches and trenches. This work went on for about two days, and then one morning when we awoke the Indians were gone.

The trenches were left; gaping holes hazardous to our children's safety, yet, after the first speculation as to where the men had gone, we forgot all about them. There were more imperative matters with which we had to concern ourselves.

17

One evening, a little group of people gathered in our kitchen and the conversation turned inevitably to the fact that the tank defences laid the village open to the danger of attack. It is hard to say how these particular people came together at this particular time. Undoubtedly the motivation was the rising fear of the defences – a motivation sparked into life by desperation.

True, there had been occasions before when the only action had been a muffled undertone of disapproval, discontent and rejection. Now, however, there was a difference – hopes of an end to the war had burned low, then spasmodically high, but never until now had we been able to actually see that the end was an inevitable and much longed for fact.

During the months I had been in the village, groups of prisoners-of-war had met on dark evenings, but never groups of civilians; not that this gathering was large. There were perhaps ten of us, including the great-grandparents, my mother-in-law and myself. Visiting was discouraged and closed doors nowadays were usual, for it was quite certain that the comings and goings might be, and indeed were, noted and speculated upon. It was so different from the beginning of the war here in the country, where often doors stood open all night. One might casually drop in upon an acquaintance for a few moments, but there was never any certainty that such an acquaintance, friend, or even relative, might not be listening and ready to betray a carelessly dropped word. Sensible people kept their opinions to themselves, fully aware that the receptive ears of Government were everywhere and those who were not sensible often learned to their cost that the most seemingly sympathetic ears were the most traitorous.

There was something, therefore, almost prophetic about this gathering together of these few, each of us with different reasons for being there. Some were driven by fear, yet bold with a boldness born of that fear; some were crushed and depressed by the past years and yet elated by the whisperings of coming relief; but all of us were driven by the same impulse, a determination to at least do something tangible, whatever the cost.

After some short discussion, we decided that if the 'iron fists' were dismantled and the tank defences moved and scattered far enough away to make reconstruction difficult, the worst of the aerial attacks used to open up the smaller defence positions might pass over. A fragile chance, true.

We hoped that the majority of villagers would be on our side if it came to a showdown, even though we had no way of being sure.

How we could manage to do the dismantling from a physical standpoint was another matter. We discussed ways and means. Suggestions were weighed and discarded and other suggestions offered. There was such an element of risk that no final conclusion seemed possible. The main danger was still in numbers, and yet a large number of men would be needed for the task.

Discussion and argument were so animated that, although we appeared fully aware, not one of us noticed that the tailor, the one who had made up the flag for me, had slipped from the room; if we had thought at all it would have been that he had probably gone to the outside lavatory. It is probable that had we not been so casual, the whole plan might have failed, for immediately we would have thought he had gone to betray us.

We were, therefore, quite surprised when the door was quietly opened and he walked in again. Immediately we started questioning him. He was dirty, one sleeve of his jacket was ripped and his face was white. But his eyes were shining as he said, shakily, 'You can forget the iron fists, they'll do no more damage.'

With that he sat down and picked up the bottle of schnapps from the table and took a long pull at it.

'I needed that,' he smiled, as the potent spirit brought some of the colour back to his face.

He had dismantled the grenades alone, slipping from one defence barrier to the other, quietly and unobtrusively, taking advantage of shadows which could hide one man but would give away two or more, knowing that were he caught only he would have suffered the consequences. This example of what could be done did more to consolidate our plans than anything else.

There now remained the removal of the enormous tree trunks which, balanced on the top of each other, formed a fence blocking the roads into the village.

Spurred on by this man, others went to work and each morning during the next week the barriers diminished in size. How they did it, I don't know. There must have been some noise and carts must have been used because of the size of the trees. But if the people in the houses on the outskirts of the village where these barriers were heard anything, they gave no sign, and it is probable that they were only too glad to see the danger removed.

I was reminded of the old smuggler's song:

If you wake at midnight and hear a horse's feet
Don't go drawing back the blind or looking in the street.
Them as asks no questions isn't told a lie
Watch the wall my darling, while the gentlemen go by.

Finally the last remnants of the barricades were removed and the fact that nothing was made of the dismantling is an indication of the true feelings of the villagers.

Almost immediately aeroplanes began to fly low over the houses, reconnoitring to see whether resistance would be shown or not.

It was about two weeks before Whitsun, and after a day of nerve-racking waiting we felt that we would be safer in the forest during the night. We packed Michael and Christopher in the handcart. They were warmly dressed and rolled up in blankets. Between them we packed everything we felt necessary for emergencies. We stuffed food down the corners of the cart and left the house.

Through the village we plodded. It was already late in the evening, and although it was difficult to make out faces as we passed, it was obvious that others had the same intention. There was a regular procession and caravan of ghostly figures; no words were spoken, only now and again a child started crying, to be hushed almost immediately.

I pushed the truck, my mother-in-law walked alongside it, and the old folks brought up the rear. We were very afraid when we reached the last of the houses in the village; we stopped. We could hardly believe what we saw. Dozens of handcarts were standing in front of a house, but the owners of the carts had disappeared. Only those immediately in front of us and those bringing up the rear could be seen. There were not many of those behind us as we lived the furthest point away.

The last house in the street was that of Forester Kolb, and as we reached it he came out and begged us not to go on into the forest. 'There are Moroccans in there,' he said.

Our blood ran cold; we had heard that this section of the French Army when fighting would kill without hesitation or reason whatever they saw moving.

I think, although we all realised that the Allies were on their way and near, none of us could believe they were quite as near us as that.

Herr Kolb opened the door. 'Bring the children in quickly,' he called. 'You can stay here.'

Inside was a pitiful sight – seated on the floors against the walls and even on the middle floor space were about fifty people. Most of them were either very young or very old, all of them white, drawn and obviously terrified. Some of them were invalids who had been carried to what they hoped would be safety by their relations.

A few of the older ones grumbled softly at having been brought from their beds, they couldn't realise why they were there; mothers prayed softly, and others just sat with the hopeless stares of the despairing. We sat there until about five o'clock in the morning, during which time one tiny girl, who had been brought from her sick bed, died of pneumonia in her mother's arms. There was nothing any of us could do.

The boys slept; they had always proved themselves adaptable. But great-grandfather grumbled, 'What are we here for anyway ... stupid ... stupid ... we should have stayed home in bed, they won't do anything to us ... I want my breakfast.' His muttering rose and fell on our ears until we hardly noticed it.

Gradually morning light began to soften the horror of the night. We began to wonder if we had been right in running away. By ones and twos, families stretched their stiff limbs and left the house, and the trek started again – in reverse.

When we got back to the farm we left the truck still packed and took the children indoors. We left them in their warm clothing just in case anything happened and we had to run suddenly.

All that day we waited. When aeroplanes flew over we rushed to the cellar and cringed in fear and when they passed we rushed to the front door to watch them disappear.

During the morning, a friend came to the door. She had walked from Singen, thinking she would be safer away from the town. Hilda Gless had lost her only child while it was still a baby, before the war, and her husband had been killed in Russia, so that she was now quite alone. We were glad to have her with us.

In the afternoon one of us noticed a puff of smoke on the skyline, and from then on we could plainly hear the artillery as it neared us. Soon we could actually identify the farms as they were hit. It seemed as if we were the centre of a wheel which was shrinking in on us, and this is quite probably true; as having no railway station in the village or lines running through it, there seemed to be no reason to blow us out of existence. There was no moment when the house was still; it shook, rattled and vibrated all the time.

As the evening closed in and darkness fell, for there was no moon, we decided there was only one thing to do and that was that one of us must keep watch for developments throughout the night and be ready to warn the others.

The first duty fell to me. I think I was glad of this for I could not have slept or rested in case of harm coming to the boys. With night, silence fell and as I sat in the isolation of the front parlour, I could no longer hear the artillery.

It was quiet … too quiet. The whole night seemed to be holding its breath and waiting. Ears strained, I listened for the sound of aircraft and then jumped nervously, for there was a light tap on the shutters.

'Who's there?' I said as loudly as I could without disturbing anyone else in the house.

A man's voice answered, 'Can you tell us where we could rest for the night?'

I opened the front door, which we had bolted, peered into the darkness and saw three German soldiers. They told me the whole territory was surrounded and they wanted shelter until it was safe to give themselves up. They were dirty, haggard and obviously exhausted.

Making sure that no one else had been disturbed by the intrusion, I placed my candle on the table and closed the door softly behind me as I stepped out into the street.

It was so dark that I had to hold one of the soldier's hands to guide him, while the other two joined in a tail behind us. Then I led them to a farmhouse a little way distant, where I knew a farmer would take them in. In that farmhouse, too, they were keeping watch and the farmer gladly led them to his cowshed, where they bedded down for the night.

But it didn't stop there. No sooner was one batch of soldiers accommodated than others appeared as if from nowhere, all asking for shelter. By the time morning came there must have been not a few short of a hundred or more who emerged from various cowsheds with straw, and worse, adhering to their sorry uniforms. They sat about in front of the houses and waited, some hopelessly expecting the worst, that they would be shot; some indifferent; some afraid; and most of them very young. It occurs to me now that in those days nearly all expectations were negative.

A few of the men begged me to take their addresses and write to their wives to say where they had been at the end –

all of them were convinced they would not see their families again, such was the propaganda barrage to which they had been subjected.

We tried to cheer them up, although we ourselves were suffering from 'propaganditis'. One of the rumours which had been spread was that, were the Germans defeated, arrangements had been made to spread gas over the area, and a great number of the villagers believed that this would indeed happen and that there would be no escape.

Then, suddenly, the soldiers were gone; one moment it seemed that they were spread thickly about the roadside and grassy areas, and then all was quiet. It had been clear that had these men walked away from the village in any direction they would have walked straight into the advancing troops, and their disappearance indicated that the advancing patrols were much closer than was apparent.

The dull rumble of artillery had turned to a continuous roar by now, and puffs of smoke from direct hits could be identified as nearby farms owned by people we knew.

We had been advised by the *Bürgermeister* to bury any spirits and valuables because of possible looting and because of the danger of drunkenness among the French soldiers who might be billeted in the village once they had penetrated that far. That day we spent digging a hole in the vegetable garden into which we carefully placed the bottles of schnapps and liqueur which we had in the house, as well as various valuables. The digging of the hole was not difficult, but the trick lay in replanting vegetables in the newly turned earth and watering them properly to ensure that they did not obviously droop in that particular area.

When it got dark we crept out with the firearms we had in the house. The two rifles and a small revolver, which we had kept handy for emergencies, were no longer safe to keep because there would undoubtedly be a thorough search made of every house. The revolver we buried under an apple tree in the orchard along the road leading past the lake. The rifles we threw into the lake, and we discovered later that we were not the only ones to do so. The fishes must have wondered indeed

147

at the metallic feast being thrown to them that night.

We thought that at the speed with which the Allies were closing in, they would have taken possession of the village much sooner. Now that they were so near, they seemed to move very, very slowly and the tension of wondering what Baumann and his one or two friends might do made us all the more anxious that relief should come quickly, in whatever form.

The next day a neighbour's wife, whose husband had been on duty on the German side of the Swiss border, came to tell us that her husband had returned home. The guards, with their guard dogs, had been taken away from the border – or perhaps they had deserted their posts, knowing the end was so close.

The border on the German side was open at last. This was the opportunity I had been looking for to get myself and the children into Switzerland, where I had friends, and thence home to my parents.

With this in mind I went to see Father Stroebel and asked him if he could get me transport. He readily agreed and took me to a farmer who offered to drive us as far as the now open border. There was only one stipulation: that once he had begun driving there must be no getting down from the cart, no matter what happened, until we were at our destination.

We had to move quickly and it was no more than an hour later when the cart stopped in front of our house and we loaded a few belongings into it. I climbed to the front with the driver. Michael sat on one knee, Christopher on the other, and with their heads close together in an effort to ensure that, should there be an air attack, we would all be killed together, we drove off. Those we left behind were in tears but I felt like an automaton with no emotion – it was all so unreal, so impossible.

As the cart moved down the road towards Singen, aeroplanes flew over, some of them so low we thought they must strike the trees on either side of the road. The children were too scared to move and we kept on going until we arrived at an intersection. To the left lay Constance, to the right, Singen.

Suddenly there was a roar as a motorcycle sped towards us from the direction of Singen. As it came closer we identified it as a French outrider. He stopped the wagon and asked us where we were headed. I tried to explain to him that we were British and that I was trying to get into Switzerland, but he couldn't understand and, shaking his head vigorously, he indicated that French troops were close behind him and that we should only run into trouble if we continued.

The wagon turned and started back to the village. This time the tears did run down my cheeks; so close to freedom and yet we were still so far away. Had we got through that day, I feel we would have been spared much hardship, for our journey to England eventually took us eleven weeks.

My mother-in-law was happy to see us again, and clutched the boys to her as if she would never let them go again.

18

We had left in the evening of one day and returned in the morning of the next; that afternoon the first motorcycles ridden by the French military roared into the village, followed by lorries and, lastly, the infantry.

We retrieved our Union Jack from beneath the kitchen cupboard where we had hidden it and hung it over the front door. It was only a couple of hours later that two French officers came to our door. They told us that they were arranging for quarters for their men and that many residents would have to move out of their houses altogether, although, in general, most of them were given leave to occupy one or two rooms so that they could cook and look after those comfortably housed in the other rooms.

They, of course, questioned the Union Jack, and I explained as best I could in what, at that time, was my 'school' French. As a consequence, they allowed me, the children and my mother-in-law, who in any case always shared the bedroom on the ground floor, to remain in it. Great-grandmother and grandfather, though, had to move out of their rooms upstairs and bed down in the kitchen, while the two officers decided they would personally quarter themselves upstairs as a 'protection' for us. In the event we were glad of the arrangement for they did actually protect us from being bothered by the soldiers, who commenced stealing anything they could lay their hands on.

I was taken to the village hall to report to the French Commander, and after discussing the matter with me, his English being far better than my poor French, he assured me that we would be 'looked after'. What that meant I had no idea.

The officer came to the door of the village hall to see me off the premises and there an amazing sight greeted us. Passing by was a procession that reminded me of a circus parade. There were in it Moroccans in all types of dress, undress and uniform. Behind them came open trucks hung with pots and pans and other odds and ends, all being pushed by a gaudily clad array of Moroccan women and girls. All of them were completely uninterested in either us or anything else around them. Their sole purpose in life seemed to be to keep pace with their menfolk marching ahead. The Commander told me the women cooked and cared for that section of the troops and that a French guard would not be safe in quarters with them at night. As a consequence they would have to be put in the village jail at night to protect not only the local residents, but also the French themselves.

I wondered and shuddered at what might have happened had we gone into the forest the previous night, instead of stopping at the forester's home.

When I returned to the house I found the kitchen table filled with packages. Investigation revealed several pounds of meat, butter, sugar, cereals and bread. It was unbelievable.

As I stood looking at the munificence, a farmer friend of ours came in and placed another parcel with the rest. The man had always been a friendly person, but now he had changed. He bowed and stuttered about being sorry there was only three pounds of butter in the parcel and that he would bring another pound later. It was mystifying and it took me quite a long time to assure him that I knew nothing about any butter. I then offered to pay him ... and finally when he refused, I discovered that the Commander had given the order that certain farmers were to deliver the food to me.

It was most embarrassing; particularly as they would, and dared not, accept any recompense. It did, however, indicate that most of the farmers had different commodities stored away and had not accounted accurately to the authorities.

A curfew was set for 6 p.m. each day and for a few days life went on quietly. Each house was required to pin to its front door the names and relationships of the occupants ... and

151

this too revealed many an up to now well-kept secret.

The few Serbians and Poles, Jacques' wife and myself were sent for and questioned about firearms in the village and asked if we had received ill-treatment during the time we had been living there. A few of the Party members were marched off to Singen, together with the *Bürgermeister*, then all was again quiet.

Gradually reports began to come in from outlying farms that Russian prisoners-of-war who had been freed from the camp near Singen had started looting and threatening farmers with guns. They wanted schnapps. They were a rough, uncouth crowd, very different from the gentle Russian girls who had visited us for so many months. Finally, the breaking into the farmhouses and the shooting became so bad the French troops were forced to make a house-to-house search and round up the Russians.

Each day, the French searched the woods for Germans who were trying to escape, or the few who had been in barracks in Germany and were making desperate attempts to get home to their families. It was dangerous to be on the streets after six o'clock but occasionally one of the weary men would creep into his home after dark by a back way and be safe for a while. Uniforms were hurriedly discarded and burned and civilian's clothes put on in their place. Some who had to travel further would ask for shelter at a house of some acquaintance who they hoped would shelter them for a night and assist them in their travels to places much further afield.

As a British national I was allowed out of the village, and that solved one or two problems. The villagers brought me small bags of grain, which I took to the mill in Beuren, a few miles distant, on my bicycle. The way led through dangerous woods, but I was lucky in that I met none of the soldiers or those for whom they were searching. I also collected prescriptions for village residents and surrounding farmers being treated by the doctor, and took them to Singen to be made up.

On one such trip I was cycling along the road when I came to a tree lying across it, in a heavily wooded area. A few Russians were standing beside it. I got off my bicycle, wheeled it around the end of the tree, greeted them and rode off. I did the same when I returned later on with the basket in front of my handlebars filled with drugs and bottles of medicine. The Russians made no attempt to stop me, yet on that same day another woman from a farm nearby was murdered at the barricade, and by the same Russians.

Again I was being protected by some higher force.

During those days I was always getting calls from one farm or another to come quickly when the soldiers were stealing chickens or food from the farmers. Several times I managed to talk to the soldiers in my very inadequate French and persuade them to take less than they were demanding, even in one instance to leave with nothing. But it was difficult to cope with all the problems. In general, the soldiers were quieter than we had anticipated, but there were always a few who caused trouble and of course always a few girls who asked for it.

After a few days we were informed that all nationals from the West must leave Germany. I, of course, disregarding German law, clung to the fact that I had a British passport which had been taken from me. There was some query about Michael and Christopher because they had been born in Germany, but because they were so small they were allowed to go with me.

On Whitsun weekend, I had just put my washing to soak, to be washed on Monday morning, when I was told we were to leave early on Sunday morning. It was raining heavily and it was a problem to get the clothes dry in time to pack – still dirty, of course.

In my innocence and thinking that the move to England would be simple and fast, I packed, in all, seven cases, one of them an iron-bound wheat chest. In one of the cases, a small one, I packed food and bottled milk, which we first sterilised; this would, I thought, last us for the journey. On Sunday morning we were transported in a bus to Constance and on to the frontier.

How happy we were! Going home at last!

Little did we know what lay before us.

PART TWO

THE LONG JOURNEY BACK

ELEVEN WEEKS OF HELL

19

We were driven in an open lorry to an hotel in Constance to wait until the Swiss barrier was opened. The frontier at that point cut through one of the main streets of the town, at right angles. Beyond the German barrier it was about fifty yards to the Swiss border. On both sides life had continued uninterrupted throughout the war, but people who had once been neighbours on the same street were separated from each other for the duration of it; between them were the watchful guards.

On the very few occasions I had been in Constance I had longed to get across – it was such a short distance and yet freedom was so far away, an absolute impossibility.

Now we were to cross that barrier and, as I now thought, in a few hours, two days at the most, we would be home. The hotel where we were unloaded from the lorry was packed with people. Transports from every direction had been and were still being brought in, some from long distances away. There were Belgians, French and many Dutch, and nationals from many other countries – but I saw none at that point from Britain. Several nuns were busy ministering to any who needed attention for there were sick and injured amongst them.

None of those sitting around waiting for something – anything – to happen knew how they would get to their destinations and, of course, speculation was rife.

Christopher, who was twenty-two months old, got into trouble right away. Always full of energy, he kept on running around until finally he slipped and fell, cutting his head on the ribs of a radiator There was no adequate means of stitching the wound and he bears the scar to this day; a piece of sticking plaster had to suffice to stem the bleeding.

At last the motley crowd, all chattering gaily at their

157

newfound freedom and the thought of returning home, were told to move toward the frontier gates. They were opened and we walked through, leaving behind us those with whom we had spent the last hard years. Somehow my seven cases were taken across by the willing hands of those around us.

One of them was a wheat chest, wooden and banded with metal; there was a large yellowish leather suitcase; a smaller weekend dark brown leather case with my initials 'A.J.U.S.', given to me on my twenty-first birthday by my parents; an attaché case containing two bottles of sterilised milk, Christopher's feeding bottle and some bread; a briefcase with papers; a roll of two rugs strapped, which small Michael carried and a wooden box about three inches square, nailed closed, containing Michael and Christopher's baby clothes.

In addition, slung around my neck the boys' small white enamel potty. Later I was to bless the thought which had added that to my load. What I'd have done without it in the awful conditions in which we found ourselves, I'll never know.

I had also, just prior to leaving, cut out two pieces of leather four inches square and on those had printed in indelible ink the boys' names; my parents' address in England; their birth dates; my name and, in the case of Christopher, the formula he was taking night and morning. These I hung around their necks with string. I'd seen so many mothers, escaping in front of the Russian advance as it moved further and further into Germany, looking for children who had become lost in the crowds of escapees. I was determined we would stay together come what may. I had also hung two leather belts from my coat, which attached to the boys at the other ends. It was terribly awkward but I was taking no chances.

We walked into a world of peace in Switzerland, almost unable to believe what was happening. The quiet and strangeness awed us. Now, with two sets of barriers and guards behind us, the chattering ceased and it seemed as if we were testing the texture of the ground as we slowly moved along the short distance along the road to the field in which a refugee camp had been set up.

Enormous marquees had been erected in the field, each

158

bearing the name of a different country: BELGIUM, NETHER-LANDS, FRANCE etc. The crowd gradually thinned as each person headed towards his or her designated spot. But there was no marquee labelled 'BRITAIN' and, not knowing what to do next, I sat down on the grass in the centre of the camp with my boys and waited.

Presently a Swiss officer stopped in front of us. He turned out to be the commander of the camps. I didn't know it then, but that man proved a true friend and I corresponded with him and his wife until their deaths, long after the war ended.

He was amazed to find a British national, particularly with children, in such a place and he asked if I had any friends in Switzerland. He then wrote down the name of Paul Broglie, who lived in Zürich, assuring me that he would attempt to contact him. Perhaps Paul could make arrangements to get me out of what was to become a transport into France. He told me his name – Commander Ladner. Then he led us to one of the marquees, where he said we could sleep for the night.

The floor of the marquee was spread with a thick layer of hay and he found us a place to settle down, suggesting that I sleep with one of the children on either side of me. This was a matter of security, he said, considering the unknown characters of those with whom I was sharing space. I was to follow this procedure for the rest of our journey. Fragile enough protection, but at least it gave me a moral sense of security. At least four times during the night he came in with a torch and flashed it over us to ensure we were all right.

In the morning we were lined up and taken to a station where a train stood ready for the journey into France. I had almost given up hope of seeing Commander Ladner when he appeared and said that he had telephoned Paul and that he was attempting to get permission to take us out of the transport and take us to his home in Zürich. However, we would have to wait until the train arrived at Basel, where Paul and his wife intended to meet us.

Before we left that morning Commander Ladner picked up the two boys and said he would like to be photographed with them. This caused an upset, as the boys, seeing him in uniform, thought he was going to take them away from me and they screamed and struggled in his arms. No amount of reassurance served to quiet them until they were back at my side.

Prior to our boarding the train, Commander Ladner slipped a piece of paper into my hand with his home address on it. Then we were rattled on our way.

In a very short time we arrived at the station in Basel. There we were unloaded onto the platforms, which were lined with trestle tables, each one loaded with food provided by the Red Cross.

We sat down thankfully, and I, for one, thought that if this was a sample of what was to come on the journey, then things would be very good. But that was the last proper meal we were to get for eleven weeks.

Then, as we were eating, a shadow fell across my plate and when I looked up there was Paul, with his wife Lorlie. Lorlie was in tears. They had tried all morning to get permission to take us to their home, but without success.

Before we boarded the train again for the journey into France, they gave us packages of butter, tubes of honey, cheese and some bread. They assured me they would contact my parents and tell them that we were on our way back to England. That was the last time my parents were to hear of us for four weeks.

20

We were in a compartment of the train which in my naïve thought would take us to a Channel port. I was soon disillusioned.

Several Dutch men sat with us, helped me and were quite friendly. When the train stopped at stations along the way they fetched whatever drinks or foods were being offered. But once we were in France, those offering it were doing so mainly to any French nationals in the transport and had it not been for those Dutch boys, I wouldn't have stood a chance of getting any sustenance at all.

At around midnight, the train stopped at Mulhous (Muhlhausen). We were told to get out and leave our belongings on the platform, and then we were led to an enormous building which was brightly lit. It looked as if it had been a huge department store at one time.

Now, at eighty-seven, I cannot for the life of me imagine how, with all the dumping of luggage in different locations and the very weight of it, I managed to get it all to England intact. The pressure, stress and misery of that journey have wiped my memory of most of the lifting, lugging and searching for it amongst all the mountain of packages, bags and bits and pieces of those travelling with me. I did manage to retain hold of the briefcase with some essential documents and felt that so long as I had the boys safe and the papers, all else was of little importance.

My boys were half asleep and my heart ached for them, so young yet they had endured the hardships and shocks of war, and now we were faced with yet another 'unknown' of who knew what difficulties and trials.

When I was a small child I often dreamed of standing in the

161

dark outside just such a brightly lit building. That dream, which had given me such a feeling of loss and desolation, was now reality, every detail as I remembered it. My nightmare come true.

I was told to put the boys in a small bed in the care of French Red Cross nurses, although, frankly, their painted fingernails and lipstick with heads topped with huge extravagant hair arrangements belied my idea of nurses as I had known them in England and in Germany.

All the women were then herded to another part of the building, into a huge hall divided about one third of the way by a kind of post office grille. Behind the grille stood approximately twenty men who looked as if they had just been hired after a hard day's manual labour. They wore dungarees which were not too clean, were unshaven, some even with leaves in their shirts or jackets; certainly not officials. Each of them passed us a wooden drawer. We were ordered to strip, place our clothes in the drawers and hand them back to the men behind the grille. We were horrified and embarrassed, but could do nothing but follow orders. We were then herded to the showers. There were no towels, or any means of drying ourselves, and as the pièce de resistance, an impeccably dressed Frenchman stood in the centre of the shower room, smoking a cigarette and obviously amusing himself at our discomfiture.

Out of the showers, we were each sprayed with what appeared to be delousing powder, which stuck and so became an unnecessary addition to our misery, particularly as none of us needed delousing after or even before the stinging quantities of cold water. Certainly I hadn't needed the treatment in the first place. But no one was excused and the treatment continued until we all stood like silvery white ghosts. We were then stood in a queue lining up in front of a series of 'doctors' who appeared to be giving inoculations.

Just before I reached the top of the queue someone came to tell me that Michael had fallen from the cot where they had placed him and his brother, and that he was crying; so I had to retrieve my clothing and run to him. I took him back with me, leaving Christopher sleeping. Saved from the 'delousing'.

Michael was also inoculated several times by those 'doctors'. I have no idea what those needles were for. Thank Heaven this was before AIDS raised its ugly head, for hygiene on the part of those plaguing us, and their instruments, was certainly not adhered to. And I still question why they were necessary – for surely if Michael and I were carrying germs or might become ill, so also Christopher; and, in any case, had Michael not been awakened at that time he would have been spared those dubious attentions. Finally our clothes were restored to us and it was a relief to be covered again and free from the embarrassing and amused smirks of those men.

We were then taken to another hall, where the baggage and the children were collected and we sat at small tables. It was then discovered that my briefcase carrying our papers, birth certificates etc. had been stolen.

And again the Dutch boys who had helped me with carrying the boys and luggage thus far stepped in and came to my assistance. After some amateur detective work, it was discovered in the hands of an undersized, undernourished Jew who had obviously hoped he would find something valuable.

By that time my nerves were beginning to fray and I felt that somehow I had to get official assistance. I approached one of the so-called officials who stood about among us, and told him I was British and asked if I could talk with British authorities. Would he, could he, understand? Possibly the word 'British' and maybe 'office' registered, because he led me to another large room. The only trouble was that the room was peopled with more individuals from either our or another transport; this time all were men, all stripped and undergoing the same embarrassments we women had suffered. At least they had the advantage over the women as their own sex was in charge of the boxes of discarded clothing and there was no arrogant supervisor watching proceedings.

In the office I could get no concrete advice from anyone, and certainly no one had any idea where British authorities might be, although one of them did speak English. So I returned to the children, hoping that wherever the transport was going, it would take us at least part-way in the direction of England. None of us had any idea of the intended destination of the transport, or what the French had in mind to do with us. There seemed to be no fundamental plan or order; and we were all being treated like cattle, to be dealt with wherever the officials who happened to be in any one place thought to send us.

Finally we were told we were to be moved and were all lined up in front of another of the 'post office' counters. At the first of these we had to hand over any German money in our possession. I parted with one thousand German marks and was told I would get French francs at the next counter in return. However, at the next counter all I was given was a receipt for my German money. The French members of the transport were all issued with French francs, and now all the other nationalities, Dutch, Belgians, etc. and myself, were destitute. We hadn't even enough money to buy a postage stamp, but we were told that our relatives would be advised that we were on our way. Certainly, the word 'way' didn't mean home, and I discovered later that none of those messages were sent, and the promise made was to lull us into a false sense of security.

The receipt I had received for the money provided evidence, yet it was at least two years after our return to England before the French were to refund that which they had taken from me.

Everyone was then issued with Red Cross parcels. Our first thoughts were of joy at being handed such munificence, but then I realised it would be impossible for me to carry three parcels (although they would have stood us in good stead throughout the weeks to follow). They were so bulky and heavy I had to be content with removing the smaller and most nutritious items and stowing them in my already overladen pockets. The remainder, mostly canned food, had to be discarded, although there was no lack of 'takers' among those who were not so handicapped as I was.

We were then marched back to the station and put on another train. This time all the glass in the windows of the carriages was broken or entirely missing. It was evening when we started out and the night was extremely cold. To prevent

164

the children from freezing I covered them with my own coat and then lay on top of them on the seat. One of the Dutch boys took off his leather jacket and put it over me.

The train rumbled on but we had no idea of its direction. Probably because of war damage and only temporary repair, the journey was extremely bumpy, slow and uncomfortable.

In the very early hours of the morning, the train stopped. It was to emerge that most of the moves were done during the nights, and I had to waken the boys and lift them around with my other luggage. In fact I was carrying so much I must have looked like an itinerant pedlar.

We were de-trained in the pouring rain and the darkness. Where it was we had no idea. We were rushed over the station bridge and down the other side to a street. It was now that I realised what an innocent I had been to set out with all that luggage. Each piece I had to drag up the steps and down again At the top of the steps I tied the boys with two straps to the bigger case while I went up and down lugging the rest, bit by bit, to the top – then the same procedure going down.

The unhappy and weary parade was herded outside the station into a roped-off section of pavement, where, bewildered, we were left to our own devices. No food or drink was distributed and the rain was pitiless. There was nothing and no one to alleviate the misery of the situation. There was no shelter, so I laid the boys on the top of the largest piece of luggage and covered them with my leather coat, for they were too exhausted to stand. They slept, a troubled, miserable sleep, while I stood beside them hopelessly praying for an alleviation of our plight.

Finally at daybreak there was a movement in the crowd who were also standing around us waiting, and a general exodus in the direction of a town. Clutching Michael by the hand and carrying Christopher in my arms, I plodded dejectedly along.

The Dutchmen helped me with the luggage and occasionally one of them gave Michael a lift, but for the most part the three-year-old walked stolidly at my side clutching the bundle of rugs as Christopher grew heavier to my weary limbs.

I had him wrapped in two double-sized blankets on one of

my arms and I carried the case containing their clothes in the other hand. Besides, as I have said, after my case with our papers had been stolen, I now had those stuffed in my pockets. In fact, anything necessary for the children I kept close to my person. Any offers of assistance with those items I rejected.

Looking back, it seems quite evident that it was sheer willpower that enabled me to carry so much and that in normal circumstances I could not have even moved one of the cases from the ground.

How far we walked I shall never know, for we never did discover the name of the station at which we were disembarked from the train. At last we came to another town and were herded into another station. By that time, after stops and starts throughout the day, it was night again and we were exhausted.

Still no food had been provided and had it not been for the small supplies I had brought with me and the remaining food given me by the Broglies at Basel, we would have been even worse off.

At night we stopped at another station, this time marked. It was Chalons-sur-Marne and the waiting room was our refuge for the night. The platforms had been fitted with planks raised about three feet from the ground and on these blankets were strewn, every one of them filthy and infested with fleas and other crawling vermin. There was no option or escape from them until morning, when we were loaded onto trucks and taken to a camp.

The camp consisted of a few tents and one long wooden hut containing American camp beds, set up so closely to one another that they touched. Swarming as it was with refugees and their oddments of parcels there was little room to move.

The toilet accommodation was not only primitive, it was disgusting. Not one door fitted. There were no door handles or means of closing the doors. It was here we had our first introduction to 'modern' French toilet equipment, which was merely a hole in the floor with the indentations for feet either side of it. No cistern, no seats, just the filthy hole. And privacy too was absent, for the booths were in constant use and with no means of securing the doors, they were constantly being pushed open … and often left open when the man or woman, seeing the booth was occupied, moved away frustrated. The washbasins had all lost their plugs, which barely mattered, since there was very little water. In order to give the boys even an inadequate wash I had to sit them on the plug hole and wait until sufficient water had trickled in, in order to clean them as best I could.

There we were, caught in the clutches of disorganised horror, being pushed around like cattle, with no say in the matter; with comfort of any kind gone, privacy gone, and now all hope too was gone. As for emotions, they had long since gone: no smiles, no tears, even from my little ones; nothing but the apathy that comes from hopelessness. Psychologically we had touched the bottom of the barrel and the question was, would even that give way, to sink us even deeper into the mire of despair.

Finally we were issued with meal cards, each being marked off as we were handed the 'meals', consisting of watery soup and stale bread. There was no indication as to how long we were to be quartered here and on the second day I decided to investigate outside the camp to see if there was any way of escaping. But to what or where any escape might be, I had no idea.

There is a saying in German that the devil makes man inventive. It was certainly true in my case. I had walked a considerable distance when I noticed an American flag flying outside a house which looked as if it were occupied by American soldiers and officers.

There was a lot of laughter and voices coming from a room off the hallway and, as the front door was open, we stepped inside and I knocked on the door of the room from which the noise was coming. No one answered, probably because of the noise inside, so we sat on a bench and waited – the waiting made more difficult because of the aroma of food which came from what was obviously a dining room. It would have been too intimidating to go in without invitation; and my courage level was by now too low for that.

I remember thinking how like we were to the Bisto Kids advertisement at which I had so often laughed in England. The sight of those two kids sniffing the aroma of the cookhouse will never leave me again. This was bitter reality, for we were hungry.

This fact seemed to elude those officers when they finally emerged from the room; however, the one in charge listened patiently to me; he was very sympathetic and also astonished at our plight. Then he left for a few moments and when he returned he said he had been in touch with the French officials in charge of the camp at Chalons-sur-Marne and that the Americans would provide a truck and take us back to the camp. Then they left, and my impression was that they intended taking steps to get us out by negotiating with the French; but it wasn't to be because before anything was done and the Americans were out of the way, we were promptly moved by the French on another truck to Epernay.

That was the last I was to see of the helpful Dutch.

The luggage was put on the truck already loaded with equipment – the boys were lifted up onto it and I walked beside it. Of that walk I only remember a signpost we passed marked 'To Rheims'. None of the roads pointed in the direction of home.

In Epernay we were taken to the gates of a deserted factory, built around a stable yard. Horse stables filled one side of the yard. On the other side was a huge tap, probably used at one time for washing down the yard, and there appeared to be only one toilet, if such a word could be used to describe the reeking shack built into one corner. Thankfulness that I had brought the boys' potty with me went through my mind. From the side of the shack a narrow staircase led up from the yard to what had apparently once been offices. These were bare, dirty and stripped of door handles, locks or any means of closure. There were no light fitments and no indication that any had ever existed. The staircase was exceptionally steep and was so filthy that in order to get my children up it, I had to hold their hands in mine to prevent their touching the walls or steps.

The room in which we were to be housed contained more

camp beds. The occupants of that factory must have numbered abound 150, all of them Italian men, and all extremely dirty and unshaven. Here we were to sleep, and in about an hour an Italian entered the room with a gasoline can in his hand. It was empty of gasoline although it still smelled strongly of it. He thrust his hand into it and produced three pieces of something that appeared to be cooked meat. It was unfit to be called food, and for two tiny children like mine, impossible. My first task therefore had to be to find food for them.

I discovered that the French authorities were housed in offices close to the factory and went to them to demand milk. But how to sterilise it? There seemed no way out of that dilemma, but at last one of the Italians in the factory produced a small piece of candle and a match, and I parboiled the milk, teaspoonful by teaspoonful over the candle flame.

That night we lay down to sleep, but barely had we closed our eyes than the door flew open and in came an Italian with a Bulgarian girl. They took no notice of us, but threw themselves into one of the beds in a corner, and I prayed that my little ones would not waken until morning. How we had ever come to be among such people I was unable to think. Years later, however, I could understand that the depths of apathy and misery can drive people out of themselves to be what they perhaps are not.

In the morning we were lined up in the yard and issued with a mug of acorn coffee and two hard biscuits smeared with what was supposed to be jam, and that was all. We washed at the tap in full view of everyone. There was no soap, no toothbrush, no privacy, but lots of smell from the so-called lavatory, whose contents oozed out into the runnels in the yard.

Something simply had to be done. The children couldn't exist in such conditions, so I set off on a tour of the town. It was Sunday morning and I was determined to find a church where perhaps the minister could understand English.

I did find a Protestant church and was told by a passerby that the minister was an Englishman who had to flee the German invasion.

I wandered on and soon I came to a Catholic church. At that

169

moment the congregation was leaving and I noticed among the worshippers several American GIs. Summoning my courage I approached one of them and told him of our plight. I begged him for a postage stamp so that I could write to my mother and let her know where we were. He saw that our need was greater than just one stamp and told me to meet him in a restaurant at twelve o'clock.

At a quarter to twelve we were sitting at a table. The waiter eyed us suspiciously and our hearts were beating as though we were awaiting a lover's rendezvous.

Would he come?

Bless him! He arrived on time loaded with tins of food, milk, bread and news that he had a fiancée in Nottingham, England. He would ask her to get in touch with my mother.

Cared for? Oh yes, indeed. We suffered, but we were cared for all along the way.

We went back to the factory for a few hours and then I had another idea. I called on the American military police. They had an office a short distance away. The major in charge was astounded to see a British woman and two children in such a state. He said that if the Americans had their way they would have flown us straight to England, but since they had no jurisdiction they telephoned the French authorities and demanded that we be issued with train tickets to Paris, to enable us to get to the British Embassy.

Back we went to the French, where we were issued with the necessary tickets We were told the train would not be leaving for some time and we would have to wait. The American office closed at five and about one minute to five a French official asked to check something on the tickets. Having got them in their possession again, we were whisked away in a jeep to the edge of town. From there we were marched back to Chalons-sur-Marne.

There was little strength left in us by that time. Our feet moved by sheer willpower as we plodded on. Later I learned that the American MP office, having closed at five, would not hear of our removal until it was too late to discover our whereabouts.

My only recourse seemed to be persistence, so in Chalons I went back to the house where I had seen the American officials previously. When they heard what had happened they immediately put us on a truck and drove us back to Epernay, where we were again deposited in front of that obnoxious factory.

21

It was evening when we again arrived outside the factory, and there was no chance of getting in touch with the military police. I therefore went to the French military authorities, and after an argument and (put-on) hysteria, for Michael flatly refused to go through the gates of the factory, they told me we would be housed in a château in the country.

We were given directions and started walking; anything sounded better than the factory. Our cases had to remain where they were and I doubted if I would ever see them again. However, the next day they actually appeared, loaded on an American vehicle.

Château Montflambert must have been beautiful in its day; a long, low, two-storey building that had once been a hunting lodge. Inside, everything moveable had been taken away; door handles, electric switches, even the ceiling roses. During my stay I failed to find any bathrooms or toilets, but then all the fittings had been stolen anyway. The gardens were overgrown with weeds, although there were still signs of what must have been well-kept flower beds and a small ornamental lake now overrun with loudly croaking frogs, but this was covered with water weeds.

The kitchen had ovens large enough to have catered to an army. They fitted two walls of the enormous stone-floored space and had apparently been fired by wood. They looked, and probably were, the original and undoubtedly as old as the château itself, possibly medieval. No doubt in the past many a sumptuous banquet had been produced here, although the present owners would have used more modern methods of cooking – but those too had gone. Two doors led to the basement, but they were nailed over with heavy wooden planks and I shuddered to think what could have been hidden down there. Only in the enormous dining room was there any sign of past munificence. The great marble mantelpiece was still topped by three enormous bronze figures on horseback. Perhaps they were far too heavy to have been removed by manpower; or possibly the resident family had evacuated their home too hurriedly to hide them.

I soon discovered that the soldiers quartered there were convalescents and that I was the only woman in the place. We were met at the door of the château by a crowd of these enthusiastic men, who vied with each other to take us to a room upstairs. Apart from a large number of the inevitable canvas beds provided by the Americans, the room was empty; but it had two doors, which I could see would cause a problem.

I had difficulty getting the men to leave us alone, but eventually they did, and I surveyed the situation. As usual there was no means of fastening the doors. On review it seems to me that no doors in any part of France in which we found ourselves fitted, and, of course, there were no locks either. I blocked one door with a pile of the canvas beds and put another three in a smaller pile ready to push against the other door at night time. These would, I felt, give me due warning if anyone tried to come in during the night.

The food was a little better than in the factory, since it was supplied by the Americans instead of the French. The fare was tinned hash and dried beans or peas on alternate days and very dry bread. One day a week there was a 'treat' of hard biscuit and jam. I have only to close my eyes to taste the monotony of that meagre but life-saving diet. This food was hard on my two children's stomachs, in fact downright impossible. Adding to their discomfort was that they had been used to sleeping in the dark; but here, the enormous windows were bare of coverings and since the days were relatively long, it was difficult to get them to sleep. When darkness did fall, their lullaby was usually folk songs, for each night the Serbian soldiers sang what sounded like mournful but beautiful songs as they sat on the grass in front of the building.

Two days after we arrived, I took a walk around the

grounds, and when I returned to the room I found that some-one had put some milk and eggs there. On enquiry I was told that one of the Serbians named Panitsch, had obtained them from a farmer for us, but unfortunately his motives were obvious. I needed the milk and the eggs for the children, but I wasn't prepared to sell myself for them. Panitsch could speak very little German and no English at all and I, of course, could speak no Serbian; but I managed to make him understand that his hopes were futile.

I offered to wash clothes in exchange for food for the children. A few of the men agreed to this and paid me for doing that work, and then I paid Panitsch for the food. It was an excellent arrangement and Panitsch proved a good friend. He made a primitive lock for each door of the room in which we slept and found an old donkey stove for the room. He also helped me carry Christopher to and from the nearby village, which gave us a little interest as opposed to sitting on the grass in front of the château and just waiting.

But that washing! The soldiers had recently returned from the front and their underwear was almost ready to walk away on its own. The laundry quarters, like the kitchens, must have dated back a great number of years, no doubt also put there at the time the château was built. It was an enormously dark, cold, stone outhouse with huge stone troughs to hold water. The water had to be carried from a small spring about a quarter of a mile down the road and was very cold. There was no means of heating it. I suffered a sense of disgust and nausea each time I banged, rubbed and scrubbed the distasteful articles handed to me. Yet I was at the same time grateful that, no matter how hard it was, I still had the means of survival.

As I have indicated, there were no bathrooms; the facilities for everyone were a small trench in the middle of a field beyond the lawn. A rough screen of sacking had been pegged up around it, and the only advance notice of an intrusion was gained by keeping a tiny portion of the loose flap which served as a door open with one hand to see who might be heading across the field with the loo in mind.

And waiting ... It seemed we spent our lives waiting.

Aeroplanes flew over our heads, many of them I supposed on their way to and from England. While we sat by the ornamental lake, now full of slime and frogs which created an incessant background 'music' at night, we waited. We walked to a huge apple tree full of mistletoe in the grounds, inspected it a thousand times ... and waited. We examined the ripening fruit on an ancient peach tree along the south wall of the kitchen garden ... and waited. The days dragged on.

In the meantime my mother had received a letter from the fiancée of the American soldier who had helped me in Epernay and she immediately wrote to the Queen of England explaining our plight and begging her for help in finding us. She received a reply from Balmoral Castle:

I am commanded by the Queen to apologise for the delay in letting you know that Her Majesty has caused your letter to be sent on to the proper quarter and that enquiries are being made as to the present whereabouts of your daughter, Mrs. Baun.

The Foreign Relations Department of the Red Cross hope to be able to assist her in every way possible. The Queen wishes me to say how deeply Her Majesty feels for you all and that The Queen sends you her good wishes for the future.

Yours sincerely,

Delia Peel (Lady In Waiting)

Because of the leads as to our whereabouts given by the girl in Nottingham and the Red Cross, my parents were able to communicate with me by means of daily telegrams, which they sent reply pre-paid. It must have cost them a fortune. They told me that I should have courage, that they were doing everything possible to facilitate our return home and they told me that if I could get to Paris to the British Consulate, we would be cared for. Unfortunately there was no means of my doing so.

Still the days dragged on. One day Panitsch took us to a

village restaurant and bought lemonade for the boys. As we sat there a number of Jamaican soldiers came in and heard me talking to the boys. I was trying to teach them English now so that they would understand my parents when we finally reached home. When the Jamaicans heard that I was British they became excited. They told us to stay where we were while they returned to their quarters. When they came back to the restaurant they had chocolate for the boys. It was the first chocolate they had ever seen and they loved it.

Then one day the blow fell. Château Montflambert was to be closed. Despite all my enquiries as to where we were to be taken, and despite my fears that my parents would have to search for me all over again, we were loaded onto trucks at an hour's notice. When the trucks stopped it was outside that dreadful factory again.

This time it was I who refused to go inside. Turning our backs on the place, we walked to the American military police office where we had been before; the place from which the order had been given to the French to give us train tickets to Paris, weeks before.

Had the situation not been so pitiful, I think the sight of the Major's face when he saw us again, the three miserable objects he thought were home and safe, would have been laughable.

First astonished, then angry and disgusted at the treatment we had received from the French, he refused to let us out of his sight again. An officer was sent back for our baggage, which had been dumped at the factory, and we were driven to the American mess for dinner.

It was our first real meal in a long, long time and was to be our last for an equally long time. I remember a notice on the wall stating, 'Do not take any more than you can eat'. But we didn't have the opportunity to 'take'. The waiters had heard of our plight and they piled our plates. The chicken tasted good, so very good, but our stomachs, long disused to such good fare, could not accept it all. After the meal was finished we went outside and the American soldiers took charge of Michael and Christopher and plied them with chocolate until they were sick.

When we left the mess I was handed a parcel containing about twenty pieces of cold fried chicken, rolls and butter and we were told we would not be going back to that horrible factory. A room had been engaged for us at an hotel for the night. What a luxury that was. A clean soft bed and, more important, hope.

In the morning, a truck drew up before the door of the hotel and we were helped into it. I sat with the driver and the two boys sat on the knees of some soldiers in the back. It was a long drive to Paris but I hardly noticed the countryside. I was thinking of home and meeting my parents and brother.

The driver told me that the soldiers in the back, although also Americans, were prisoners. I didn't know what they had done but I had a secret fear they might harm my boys. How foolish I was. They hadn't seen any children at close quarters for a long time and they were making up for it. They played with the boys, cuddled them and cared for them on that journey as if they were their own.

At last the truck pulled up outside the British Consulate. We were taken to a waiting room and then into another room where clerks sat behind a row of desks. The woman who interviewed me was a Mrs G, and she was certainly no humanitarian.

Mrs G told me maliciously that since I was British I could return to England that same evening if I wished. 'But send your brats back to Germany; we don't want them,' she added. I asked her where we could stay for the night and she answered, 'Sleep on the street if you like, I don't care.'

The world spun around me, but there was nothing I could do. Then, as if from the distance, I heard a voice. I turned just short of panic, and realised that a Frenchman was standing behind me, speaking in broken English. He suggested I go with him. He took my arm and led me to another part of the Consulate. What his status in the Embassy was, I don't know, and I have no idea to whom he spoke or by what authority, for we were left to wait in a small room and could hear the murmur of his voice from behind the door. Whoever it was, he must have put pressure on Mrs G, because we were told to go to a British home in a distant quarter of Paris, where we would be housed.

Needless to say, we walked. Mrs G had the last word there. She was in charge of the 'home' and had as assistants two French citizens, a man and wife who had several grown sons.

We were put in the cellar, an enormous cavern divided in the middle by a rough partition open at the staircase end. On each side of the partition was a double row of beds, each with a straw mattress. One side was for men, the other for women.

Upstairs, the rooms of the enormous house, with the exception of a locked-off apartment for the French family, were delegated to refugees. There was no privacy of any kind. At any hour of the day or night the Frenchman and his sons would walk around, study the inmates and discuss them within hearing. Among those inmates were a few young Jewish girls who were being sent to Alexandria. The girls' rooms were segregated away from the rest of the inmates and they reported having difficulty dealing with the sons of our host.

The washing and toilet facilities were abominable, and in fact two of the three toilets were nailed shut, although the doors didn't diminish the awful stench coming from them.

The food, which was served in a large dining room, consisted of watery soup with so much pepper in it that it was unsuitable for a child and it took a great deal of effort for me to swallow it. There was, however, dessert, but we never found out what it was because it was served first to a favoured table near the kitchen and there was never enough left for the rest of the tables.

There seemed to be no restriction on our movements and I found my way to the shops. A long line of people were standing outside an office which I discovered was issuing coupons for food, so I joined the queue to ask for milk for my boys. When at last I stood before the official in charge, I was told we were not eligible for food coupons. However, desperation urged me on to argue in my pitiable schoolgirl French and eventually I was given food coupons covering milk, cheese and a little butter. How I would pay for them was another question.

My next trip was to the Red Cross office, where I had more success. I was given a Red Cross parcel for Michael and an invalid's parcel for Christopher which it was decided contained passable food for such a young child. Those two parcels saved our lives, and I stretched them out as long as I could. When I returned to the 'home' I asked the Frenchman for some boiling water to make cocoa for the boys, but this he refused. I walked to a small restaurant further down the street and asked a waitress for hot water. She gave it to me gladly and from then on, until the parcels were exhausted, that is where I had to go to get water for the hot drinks.

22

All this time I was hoping to find an English church and eventually I did, only a few blocks away from the street where we were housed. It was a beautiful church with a wonderful stained-glass window over the altar, depicting our Lord with the words 'Suffer the little children to come unto Me'. That window is burned into my memory. It restored my faith that we would be brought back home.

The vicarage itself was dusty and smelled of mice. The vicar had left when the Germans came and it had stood empty for years. The furniture, books and desk equipment in the study had not been disturbed. Dust lay thick on the walls and ceilings.

When I knocked on the door of the vicarage, it was opened by a tall, thin, elderly woman named Madame Benoit. She told me she had married an Englishman in India, but whether he was alive or dead I never discovered. Her name, for one thing, didn't appear to carry out what she told me. In fact, she seemed vague about a lot of things, with cause, I was to discover later.

She said we were at liberty to come in and eat in the vicarage in return for my helping her to clean it and the church. I was so grateful for the offer, yet it so often proved frustrating. There was so much dust, as we swept it off the walls and the floor it flew up only to settle back again. But I made an effort and I daresay some inroads were made in the dirt. The upholstered furniture was another problem. An attempt at cleaning resulted in a mass evacuation of mice. I was glad I wasn't afraid of them. After completion of a thorough cleaning, the mice calmly ran back to their former comfortable quarters. What a cat's paradise that would have been.

Madame Benoit had apparently no independent means. She had been housekeeping for the vicar for a few years prior to the war and I learned later that during that time she had a bad fall, which had affected her brain so that she had been put in a nursing home. When I spoke to the vicar some years later after my return to England, he suggested that probably she had taken advantage of the chaos when the Germans entered Paris and left the nursing home, and gone back to the only home she remembered.

At this time the American soldiers had taken over the church for their services and occasionally they brought a few eatables with them. Often we would sit down to a bare table but Madame Benoit would say, 'God will provide.' In this she was right for it was at those times, inevitably, a soldier would appear with bread or a few vegetables.

Once a week the Americans had a singsong in the vicarage and I attended it although it was in the evening, which meant leaving the children asleep in the cellar at the 'home'. The GIs brought sandwiches with them – large delicious sandwiches – and I always managed to get hold of a few for the boys. What a treat that was for them. At the singsongs I played the piano for the community singing and also for a few solos. I never did find out the name of one of the singers, who the GIs assured me was a well-known opera singer. He had a wonderful baritone voice.

By that time the irregular and peculiar diet was having an effect on Christopher. He became pale and weak.

I had no writing paper and no means of writing or posting letters to enlist the aid of my parents, nor did they now know where I was. Finally when I heard of a woman who was leaving the home for England, I tore the edges off an old newspaper and wrote on them that Christopher was ill and perhaps dying, and the woman promised to mail them to my mother.

In the meantime I took Christopher to the English hospital and asked for water to add to a tin of milk I still had from his parcel to make him a bottle. The nurse was horrified. She filled a bottle with whole milk and said it was clear he was starving. It was the first time he had had milk for eleven days.

On Christopher's birthday, his second, there was nothing to eat at all. As we walked through the streets I heard an American talking behind me, and in order to attract attention I spoke loudly to the boys in English. He heard me and asked if I was from England. When I told him of our situation he gave us a small tin of cheese he had in his pocket. That was Christopher's birthday feast.

As I have said before, that so-called British 'home' was a disgrace; apart from the Jewish girls there were also a few others, quite young, living in the home, and these latter encouraged the janitor's sons, and they in turn harassed the others housed there. This, coupled with the fact that everyone in the house was desperately seeking to alleviate their own situations at no matter what expense to others, made living precarious.

Any attempt at creating order and cleanliness in the place was futile. One day I decided to turn the straw-filled ticking on the boards that served as beds and found it crawling with maggots. The toilets were so foul that one of the unhappy inmates reported it to the Salvation Army. However, on the officer's arrival to inspect the conditions, he met with a refusal to open the nailed-up doors.

We were also in danger from Madame Benoit at the vicarage, the very source whence I thought we were getting aid. It was impossible for me to carry little Christopher any more for any great distance for I was becoming too weak. Yet each time I went to the Consulate the distance had to be walked. I asked Madame Benoit if she would care for Christopher while Michael and I walked to the city. She was willing, but one day on returning I couldn't find him anywhere. She looked at me so strangely and seemed so vague when she spoke, that I was afraid. I searched and finally heard his screams coming from the church tower, where she had locked him in. No amount of questioning could bring any lucid reason from the woman. Apparently he had done nothing wrong. Indeed both Michael and Christopher were both so cowed by the awful dragging journey that, contrary to the normal two- and four-year-old chatter and fun, they were very placid, not even crying. From then on we stayed together. Conserving my strength was not worth such horror in a small boy's mind.

In the meantime my parents had not only received the notes I had sent through the lady who had offered to post them in England, but my mother had also discovered where we were through the Red Cross.

My father had between the two wars applied for British nationality and had actually sent the money to cover the cost. When World War Two broke out the negotiations were negated, although the money wasn't refunded.

Then another blow fell – because my parents' house was so close to Northolt airport, he was told that although he would not be interned he must move away. Luckily my mother's sister Carrie still lived in Finborough Road, Kensington, and she took him in. My brother was conscripted and was in the Pay Corps, so it was because of this there was room for a Belgian lady attached to the Belgian Government to be housed in my parents' home. Immediately after the war ended, this lady, Helene de Moll, returned to Belgium and mother wrote to her. She asked Helen if she would try and get some money to me, and when she agreed my parents sent one thousand Belgian francs to the Belgian Ambassador in Paris. It was a relief when the Ambassador sent for me and handed me the money. Now at least I could buy vegetables and the few items allowed the children on their milk cards, which I had begged from the authorities earlier.

At about that time I again applied to the Red Cross for another parcel for each of the children, as I had been told when they gave me the first ones that we should be allowed one parcel per month. However, Mrs Gowan had told them that the children were born in Germany and were not entitled to such parcels. My arguments and pleas failed to produce anything for Michael, but because of Christopher's obvious weakness I was given another invalid's parcel for him.

At home in England, my brother had also been trying to help. When he heard the desperate appeal I had made to my parents he went to his commanding officer in Reading. After hearing the story he said he would try to send my brother

183

to Paris in the line of duty, so that he could perhaps assist me.

One day the liaison officer between the Consulate and the 'home' came and told me we were to be sent to England the next Thursday. He took us to an office where we could radiogram my parents, and for a few hours we were happy. But my hopes were dashed, for the next day he said I could return to England, but the children would have to be sent back to Germany, or I could return to Germany with them.

Desperate and nearly out of my mind with misery, I decided that if we could not return home then at least we would end everything together. My faith had wavered, but God hadn't deserted us. There was an elderly lady living in the home who was somewhat touched in the head, but with sufficient sanity to stop an American chaplain who was passing the home. She told him our story.

That night he sat with us and in the morning took us all to the Consulate and asked Mrs G to put him through on the telephone to the Foreign Office in London. She refused, but when he offered to pay for the call and actually reached determinedly for the phone, she suddenly decided she had our papers after all. She riffled through the pile on her desk, produced some papers and said that we could all go to England the next day.

Without warning, he leaned over, took the papers from her and found that she had had them in her possession for two weeks. He said he felt convinced that she was holding back legitimate passes to make space on the boats for black market and illegal immigrants.

That night, the last one we spent in that 'home', was the most wonderful to me. How many years I had lain awake at night dreaming of that homecoming. Now, suddenly, it was all coming true, and when the children fell asleep I stood on the steps of the home and gazed at the stars, hardly daring to believe that in the next few hours I would be really in England.

At four o'clock in the morning I awoke Michael to dress him for the journey. But he was afraid of leaving his brother behind and insisted that first I dress Christopher.

184

We climbed the stairs from the cellar for the last time and manhandled that dreadful load of luggage into a truck for the ride to the Gare du Nord, whence we left for Le Havre. It will probably be amazing to the reader, and it is amazing to me, that all this time I was still carting about those seven pieces of luggage, including the wooden box, roped up for safety, which contained some of the children's clothing for the winter.

When the driver of the truck unloaded us we found a long queue of people waiting to go through a checkpoint before they were allowed on the boat. I was standing with the boys behind a sailor and just before we got to the head of the queue he picked up the roped case and said, 'I'll get this through for you – they won't open it if I have it.' He was right. We got through easily and got on the ship.

From there we could see the whole of the port, and what a sight that was! Wrecked ships sticking out of the water, bombed buildings on the land and the sea littered with rubble.

Although the ship was enormous, when we got on board we found it packed to probably over-capacity. We lucky ones sat on the deck. Then just as the ship cast off, the captain announced that lifebelts would not have to be worn, since it was *thought* that all mines had been cleared from the Channel. However, he showed us where the belts were, in case we did strike a mine. All the women, including myself, immediately grasped their children and hung on to them tightly for the crossing.

Never in my life have I had such keen vision. The grey line of England on the horizon as we neared the coast was visible to me long before I would normally have seen it, and my tears could not be held back. Tears I had not shed during the whole of the war came now from a full heart. This was England, my England, home and heaven all rolled into one.

As the ship docked, we stood at the top of the gangway waiting to leave it. A kindly sailor then picked up Michael and Christopher, one in each arm, and carried them ashore. I could just make out my mother and sister-in-law standing behind a barrier. And then, suddenly, I became aware of our condition.

My shoes had no soles and the uppers were tied on with string. Our clothes hadn't been washed for weeks and I was so weak that I walked very slowly, with my head down for shame, towards the barrier.

When I reached it a kind of hysteria seized me and I dropped the children's hands and tried to get hold of my mother until a firm hand took hold of my arm, and an English bobby said, 'You can't do that 'ere, ma'am! You'll have to go through Customs first.'

He led us to a door and handed us over to the officials, and the questioning began. At the first question my memory left me. I couldn't even remember the day I was born – I collapsed. They took me to a first-aid station and the boys were taken to my mother, who could hardly wait to throw her arms around them.

Poor mother! The children didn't know her and to them she was a complete stranger. So they cried and screamed at being taken from me. All was well, though, because mother had always had a way with her, and she soon quietened them and dried their tears.

They had to wait for me, and during that time a troopship arrived at the dock and some of the soldiers on board threw bars of chocolate to the boys. That kindness was the climax ... the children became sick. What a first meeting that was for a grandmother and her two grandsons!

At last I was revived sufficiently to get me through Customs and on the last train of the day, and we set off for Victoria Station in London. By that time everything was becoming more bewildering and unreal to me. As long as I had held the reins I had been capable. Now I had handed them over to my mother, or rather she had simply taken them from my two hands, I was no longer capable of carrying the load of misery.

I have a vague impression that during the journey mother and my sister-in-law cleaned us up – I do remember them taking off my tattered shoes and putting others on my feet. It turned out that they had been warned of what our condition might be by the Government officials who advised them of our arrival. Not only were they told that our clothing might be

186

in a desperate condition, but also that deprivation made it necessary not to give us too much to eat or unsuitable food which would cause our stomachs to reject it.

My impression of Victoria Station was the high arches, a general sense of gloom and a procession of people apparently without purpose. Overwhelmed, I stood and gazed stupefied at the throng of hurrying people. Even when my mother told me my brother was coming with a car to meet us, it didn't penetrate my confused mind.

As we stood there waiting, the crowd seemed to split apart and from a long distance away I saw two figures hurrying with a definite purpose. I could see them cutting through the crowd, each trying to get to me before the other. My dear father and my brother. What a welcome that was! Too much for my frayed nerves, and the children's too, for that matter. We were all three weak and ill. The car drove through the darkened streets of London, through familiar places which had become unfamiliar to me, and then we drew up before the centre of all my dreams ... HOME!

Christopher had fallen asleep in my arms during the drive, and I lifted him out of the car and was halfway up the path to the front door when my mother put her hand on my arm. 'Stop ... just a moment,' she whispered. Then I realised why, for from every door on the street and from every window light was glowing, and before each the neighbours stood waving a welcome to us.

EPILOGUE

It was many weeks before I was strong enough to take up the responsibilities of raising my sons. During that time I was financially reliant on my parents. Gradually, however, I recovered physically from my ordeal, and my memory, which had failed me on my entry to England, began to return. Slowly and painfully it brought back the misery of the past six years. Oddly enough, I could remember only the first letters of names and places, even then. These had to be slowly puzzled out by a long-winded process of juggling with the alphabet.

When I became well enough it became imperative that I find work to support myself and the children, and I was lucky in the fact that it was possible for me to live with my parents and that my mother was able to care for them during the day. I worked as a translator of patents in London for a time, and later as secretary in the tea-testing department of Lyons, the tea and coffee blenders, in Greenford.

Then early in 1947 my father received a letter from a young man who might be termed my step-second cousin. His grandmother was my father's step-sister. The letter was written in German, which although my father's mother tongue, he had, after so many years, almost forgotten. It was left to me, therefore, to translate and then to answer.

Kurt was a prisoner-of-war in Lancashire. We obtained permission to visit him and after some time succeeded in getting him transferred to a camp closer to our area. As restrictions relaxed he was able to visit us for short periods, although even then there were problems, for prisoners-of-war were not allowed on public transport, and the distance was too far to walk. We surmounted this difficulty by my cycling to the camp. On the return journey I took a bus and he rode the bicycle.

On one occasion when Christopher had a birthday party we attempted to obtain permission for Kurt to attend, without success. Not wanting him to miss out on the goodies, the children and I went to the camp and passed them through the barbed wire.

He was one of the first prisoners-of-war to be released in England, one of the conditions being that he worked on the land. His home was in the east zone of Germany and in due course he received a letter from the Government there inviting him to return, with promises of work with excellent conditions. He ignored it, preferring to live in exile than under communist rule.

We were married in 1947.

In 1950 our third son, Robin, was born; and shortly afterwards Kurt decided to legally adopt Michael and Christopher. An interesting feature of this adoption was that I had also to adopt my own sons at the same time. Realising the variance in law in our two countries, we applied not only to the British courts but also to the German Embassy in London, where we were told we would first have to obtain a death certificate for my first husband, Carl. In order to obtain this Carl's mother had to be contacted, and we were told that she had advised that Carl was still alive in a prisoner-of-war camp in the Ural mountains. She had, she said, received this information from another prisoner-of-war, recently freed from Russia, who had seen him.

However, research by the German authorities proved that the man reputed to have seen Carl had never existed except in the imagination of my mother-in-law. We were given a death certificate and in 1952 Michael and Christopher were adopted legally and their names changed to Franke.

Both Michael and Christopher were never in any doubt as to what they wanted to be when they left school. Michael wished to learn forestry and Christopher wanted to be a pilot. There was little outlet for forestry in England, and because he was born in Germany and his father had been German, we were told Chris could not enter the Royal Air Force.

We decided to emigrate.

189

In 1957 we came to Canada and settled in Cobourg, Ontario. Unfortunately, although Michael obtained his diploma as a forester, there was, at the time he graduated, very little permanent work in this field. Because of this he joined the Canadian Armed Forces in the Military Police.

Christopher joined the Air Cadets and won his 'Wings' by means of a scholarship through the Rotary Club. Always sports-minded, and track and field champion at high school, he confounded our advice that he had better study more than he played sports, as we thought he would never earn his living by running. He, too, joined the Armed Forces and became a physical instructor.

Both boys are married, Michael with two little girls and Christopher with two small boys. Note: Michael has since divorced and married again, and now has two sons from that marriage.

Many people have voiced the opinion that few could have come through the hardships of that return journey to England. I deny this.

Call it courage or determination, I believe that any man or woman, however weak, however lonely, however helpless, can and will survive any hardship providing there is love great enough for someone even weaker: a child. For a loved child or children a woman will battle through any dangers or hardship with the help of God. For I know now that although many times during those years I felt I was very much on my own, there was no time when I really was alone, for God had been with us all the time.